Dear Reader,

Thank you so much for purchasing "The Realtor's Mortgage Companion." I understand that real estate can be a challenging industry, and I truly believe that knowledge is the key to success.

I sincerely hope that you find this book helpful in your communication with loan officers and in your ability to guide your clients through the complexities of the mortgage process. My goal is to provide you with practical insights and strategies that will empower you to close more deals and achieve greater success in your real estate endeavors.

Wishing you all the best on your journey, and may this book serve as a valuable resource in your professional arsenal.

Cheers,

Corey Ramsey

The Realtor's Mortgage Companion

Empowering Realtors to Navigate the Complexities of Home Financing and Enhance Client Success in the Real Estate Market

by
Corey Ramsey

Contents

Introduction

In the dynamic world of real estate, where every transaction involves significant financial decisions, the role of a realtor extends far beyond merely showing properties and facilitating contracts. One of the fundamental pillars of real estate expertise lies in understanding mortgage loans and their implications for clients. This guide explores the profound importance of this knowledge for realtors, outlining how it empowers clients, builds trust, navigates challenges, identifies opportunities, facilitates smooth transactions, and maintains competitiveness.

Firstly, realtors serve as trusted guides for their clients, especially during the crucial stage of securing financing. Understanding mortgage loans enables realtors to empower clients with knowledge, ensuring they make informed decisions aligned with their financial goals and circumstances. By explaining various loan options, terms, and implications, realtors play a pivotal role in demystifying the often complex world of mortgage lending, instilling confidence and clarity in their clients' minds.

Moreover, a deep understanding of mortgage loans fosters trust between realtors and their clients. Clients rely on realtors to act in their best interests throughout the homebuying process, including selecting the most suitable financing option. Realtors who exhibit proficiency in mortgage lending not only inspire trust but also establish themselves as credible advisors capable of navigating the intricacies of the financial aspect of real estate transactions.

In addition to client empowerment and trust-building, knowledge of mortgage loans equips realtors to navigate challenges effectively. The mortgage landscape is subject to constant change, with evolving regulations, fluctuating interest rates, and shifting lending criteria. Realtors who stay abreast of these developments can anticipate potential obstacles, address concerns preemptively, and collaborate seamlessly with lenders to overcome challenges and ensure successful transactions.

Furthermore, understanding mortgage loans opens doors to diverse opportunities for realtors. Whether catering to first-time homebuyers, investors, or luxury property purchasers, realtors who possess comprehensive knowledge of mortgage lending can tailor their services to meet diverse client needs and preferences. This versatility not only expands their clientele but also enhances their marketability and relevance in an increasingly competitive real estate landscape.

Additionally, proficiency in mortgage lending facilitates the smooth execution of real estate transactions. By proactively addressing financing-related issues, coordinating effectively with lenders, and ensuring compliance with mortgage requirements, realtors contribute to seamless transactions that culminate in satisfied clients and successful closings. This ability to streamline the process adds value to the realtor-client relationship and reinforces the realtor's reputation as a trusted advisor and competent facilitator.

Finally, understanding mortgage loans is indispensable for realtors aiming to stay competitive in the ever-evolving real estate industry. In today's market, where knowledge is a powerful differentiator, realtors who invest in understanding mortgage lending gain a significant edge over their peers. By offering comprehensive mortgage expertise, realtors position themselves as indispensable partners to their clients, capable of delivering superior service and driving positive outcomes.

The importance of understanding mortgage loans for realtors cannot be overstated. From empowering clients and building trust to navigating challenges, identifying opportunities, facilitating transactions, and maintaining competitiveness, this knowledge forms the cornerstone of success in the real estate profession. Realtors who prioritize learning about mortgage lending not only enhance their professional capabilities but also elevate the standard of service they provide, ultimately leading to greater client satisfaction and long-term success.

In this comprehensive guide, real estate professionals will embark on a journey to deepen their understanding of mortgage loans and their pivotal role in the homebuying process. Each chapter in this book is designed to equip realtors with the knowledge and tools necessary to navigate the complex landscape of mortgage lending, empowering them to better serve their clients and achieve success in their careers. Here's a brief overview of the chapters covered:

Chapter 1 - Fundamentals of Mortgage Loans

This chapter introduces the fundamental concepts of mortgage loans, covering topics such as loan types, terms, and basic terminology. It provides readers with a foundational understanding of how mortgage loans work, laying the groundwork for subsequent chapters.

Chapter 7 - Mortgage Rates and Interest

Equips realtors with an in-depth understanding of the vast array of home financing options, including traditional banks, mortgage brokers, credit unions, private lenders, online platforms, government programs, nonprofit organizations, seller financing, and peer-to-peer lending. It aims to enhance realtors' ability to advise clients effectively, ensuring they make informed decisions tailored to their financial needs and homeownership aspirations.

Chapter 3 - Preparing Clients for Mortgage Pre-Approval

Chapter 2 focuses on the importance of preparing clients for the mortgage pre-approval process. It outlines the steps involved in obtaining pre-approval, discusses the documentation required, and offers strategies for helping clients improve their creditworthiness.

Chapter 4 - Understanding Mortgage Documentation

This chapter delves into the various types of documentation required for the mortgage application process. It provides insights into the purpose of each document, tips for organizing paperwork, and guidance on how to ensure documentation accuracy and completeness.

Chapter 5 - Navigating the Mortgage Application Process

Chapter 4 guides readers through the mortgage application process, from initial application submission to closing. It covers key milestones, potential challenges, and best practices for streamlining the application process and minimizing delays.

Chapter 6 - Mortgage Loan Programs and Options

In Chapter 5, readers explore the diverse array of mortgage loan programs and options available to home buyers. The chapter examines various loan types, eligibility criteria, and benefits, empowering readers to make informed decisions based on their financial circumstances.

Chapter 7 - Mortgage Rates and Interest

This chapter focuses on mortgage rates and interest, explaining how they impact loan affordability and overall cost. It discusses factors influencing interest rates, strategies for securing favorable rates, and considerations for choosing between fixed and adjustable-rate mortgages.

Chapter 8 - Handling Mortgage Challenges and Pitfalls

Chapter 7 addresses common challenges and pitfalls encountered during the mortgage process. It offers strategies for mitigating risks, navigating obstacles, and overcoming hurdles to ensure a smooth and successful transaction for both realtors and clients.

Chapter 9 - Communicating Effectively with Loan Officers

This chapter explores the importance of effective communication between realtors and loan officers. It provides guidance on building strong relationships, facilitating collaboration, and leveraging open communication channels to enhance the mortgage process.

Chapter 10 - Educating Clients on Mortgage Options

Chapter 9 delves into the essential role of realtors in educating clients on mortgage options. It discusses various loan programs, strategies for simplifying complex concepts, and techniques for empowering clients to make well-informed decisions aligned with their financial goals.

Chapter 11 - Staying Updated on Mortgage Industry Trends

The final chapter emphasizes the importance of staying abreast of mortgage industry trends. It offers insights into avenues for staying informed, such as industry publications and professional development events, and provides strategies for adapting to evolving market conditions.

By mastering the topics covered in these chapters, real estate professionals will enhance their expertise, build stronger client relationships, and elevate their success in the competitive real estate market.

Chapter 1

Fundamentals of Mortgage Loans

In the dynamic landscape of real estate transactions, effective communication between realtors and their clients is paramount. A crucial aspect of this communication revolves around mortgage loans, the financial backbone of homeownership. Understanding the various types of mortgage loans empowers realtors to guide their clients through the complexities of the homebuying process, address their concerns, and facilitate informed decision-making.

Mortgage loans are not one-size-fits-all; they come in diverse types tailored to meet the specific needs and financial situations of borrowers. For realtors, this understanding serves as a cornerstone for providing personalized recommendations to their clients. By assessing individual circumstances such as down payment funds, income stability, and eligibility for specialized loan programs, realtors can tailor their mortgage loan suggestions to align with their clients' unique requirements.

Education is key in the real estate journey, and realtors play a pivotal role as educators for their clients. Armed with knowledge about the different types of mortgage loans, realtors can demystify the complexities of the lending process and empower their clients to make informed decisions. From explaining the nuances between fixed-rate and adjustable-rate mortgages to clarifying eligibility criteria for government-backed loans like FHA and VA loans, realtors serve as trusted advisors, guiding their clients every step of the way.

Moreover, effective communication involves addressing clients' questions and concerns about mortgage loans. Homebuyers often navigate unfamiliar territory when it comes to financing their home purchase, and realtors can alleviate their apprehensions by providing clear and concise explanations. By fostering an open dialogue and offering transparent insights into mortgage loan options, realtors build trust and confidence with their clients, fostering strong relationships that extend beyond the transaction.

Realtors also act as liaisons between homebuyers and lenders, facilitating seamless communication throughout the mortgage process. By collaborating closely with experienced mortgage professionals, realtors ensure that their clients receive personalized attention and guidance tailored to their needs. From coordinating loan pre-approval to navigating the complexities of underwriting and closing, realtors streamline the lending process, ensuring a smooth and efficient transaction for their clients.

Furthermore, staying abreast of market trends and developments in the mortgage industry is essential for realtors. With a finger on the pulse of the market, realtors can adapt their strategies and recommendations to leverage emerging opportunities and navigate potential challenges. Whether it's capitalizing on favorable interest rates, identifying financing incentives, or exploring innovative loan programs, realtors who are well-versed in mortgage loan dynamics position themselves as trusted advisors, guiding their clients toward successful homeownership.

Effective communication between realtors and their clients hinges on a thorough understanding of mortgage loans. By leveraging their knowledge of the various types of mortgage loans, realtors can provide personalized recommendations, educate their clients, address their concerns, facilitate communication with lenders, and adapt to changing market conditions. Through their expertise in mortgage lending, realtors play a pivotal role in helping their clients achieve their homeownership dreams with confidence and clarity.

A mortgage loan, commonly referred to as a mortgage, is a type of loan specifically designed for the purchase or refinancing of real estate properties, such as homes, condominiums, or commercial buildings. It serves as a financial instrument that allows individuals or entities, known as borrowers or mortgagors, to secure funding from a lender, known as the mortgagee or creditor, to acquire property while pledging the property itself as collateral for the loan.

Key Terms & Elements of Mortgage Loans

Principal: The principal amount of the mortgage loan represents the total sum borrowed by the borrower to finance the purchase or refinance of the property. It's the initial amount of money borrowed from the lender, which must be repaid over time, usually in monthly installments.

Interest Rate: Mortgage loans accrue interest, which is the cost of borrowing money. The interest rate determines the amount of interest the borrower will pay on the outstanding loan balance. Interest rates may be fixed, remaining constant throughout the loan term, or adjustable, subject to periodic adjustments based on prevailing market rates.

Loan Term: The loan term refers to the duration over which the borrower agrees to repay the loan in full. Common loan terms include 15, 20, or 30 years, although other terms may be available depending on the lender. A longer loan term typically results in lower monthly payments but may result in paying more interest over the life of the loan.

Amortization Schedule: Mortgage loans involve regular payments, consisting of both principal and interest, spread over the loan term according to an amortization schedule. This schedule outlines the specific amounts allocated to principal and interest for each payment period, with early payments primarily covering interest and later payments predominantly reducing the principal balance.

Collateral: In mortgage lending, the property being financed serves as collateral for the loan. This means that in the event of default by the borrower, the lender has the right to foreclose on the property and sell it to recoup the outstanding loan balance. The property's value acts as security for the loan, providing assurance to the lender that they can recover their investment.

Down Payment: Borrowers are often required to make a down payment, which is an upfront payment representing a percentage of the property's purchase price. The down payment reduces the loan amount and demonstrates the borrower's financial commitment to the transaction. A larger down payment typically results in lower monthly payments and may help secure more favorable loan terms.

Closing Costs: Mortgage loans typically involve various closing costs, which are fees and expenses incurred during the loan origination process. These costs may include appraisal fees, title insurance, loan origination fees, attorney fees, and prepaid expenses such as property taxes and homeowners insurance. Closing costs can vary depending on the lender, location, and specific terms of the loan.

Private Mortgage Insurance (PMI): Insurance that protects the lender in case the borrower defaults on the loan. PMI is typically required for conventional loans with a down payment of less than 20% of the home's purchase price.

Escrow: An account held by a third party (typically the lender) to collect and disburse funds for property taxes, homeowners insurance, and other expenses related to the property.

Pre-approval: A preliminary determination by a lender of the amount of mortgage loan that a prospective buyer may qualify for based on their creditworthiness and financial information.

Closing Disclosure: A document provided to the borrower by the lender at least three days before the closing of the loan that outlines the final terms and costs of the mortgage loan.

Understanding these key elements of mortgage loans is essential for both borrowers and lenders to make informed decisions and navigate the complexities of the real estate market effectively.

Exploring Mortgage Loan Options

One of the most significant decisions home buyers face is selecting the right mortgage loan to finance their purchase. With various types of mortgage loans available, each with its own features and benefits, understanding the options is crucial. Let's briefly discuss the different types of mortgage loans, including fixed-rate, adjustable-rate, FHA, VA, and others, with an emphasis on how realtors can use this information to guide and inform home buyers. These topics will be discussed in more detail in Chapter 5 of our comprehensive guide.

Fixed-Rate Mortgages: Fixed-rate mortgages offer stability and predictability, with a consistent interest rate and monthly payment over the life of the loan. This type of loan is ideal for home buyers seeking long-term affordability and protection against rising interest rates. Realtors can highlight the peace of mind and budgeting certainty that fixed-rate mortgages provide, especially for first-time buyers or those planning to stay in their home for an extended period.

Adjustable-Rate Mortgages (ARMs): Adjustable-rate mortgages feature an initial fixed interest rate period, followed by periodic adjustments based on market conditions. ARMs typically offer lower initial interest rates, making them attractive for buyers who plan to move or refinance within a few years. Realtors can educate home buyers about the benefits of ARMs, such as lower initial payments and potential savings, while also emphasizing the importance of understanding potential rate adjustments and payment fluctuations.

FHA Loans: FHA loans are insured by the Federal Housing Administration and offer low down payment options and flexible credit requirements, making them accessible to a broader range of home buyers. Realtors can highlight the benefits of FHA loans for first-time buyers or those with limited savings, including the opportunity to purchase a home with as little as 3.5% down. Additionally, realtors can explain the FHA loan limits and eligibility criteria to help buyers determine if this option is right for them.

VA Loans: VA loans are available to eligible veterans, active-duty service members, and their spouses, offering competitive interest rates and no down payment requirement. Realtors can emphasize the advantages of VA loans, such as no private mortgage insurance (PMI) and flexible underwriting standards, while also guiding buyers through the VA loan process and requirements. Educating buyers about the benefits of VA loans can help them make informed decisions and maximize their homeownership benefits.

Other Mortgage Loan Options: In addition to fixed-rate, adjustable-rate, FHA, and VA loans, there are other mortgage loan options available, such as USDA loans, jumbo loans, and specialty programs. Realtors can provide an overview of these options and help buyers understand their unique features and eligibility requirements. By equipping buyers with knowledge about the full range of mortgage loan options, realtors empower them to make informed decisions and find the right financing solution for their needs.

Understanding the different types of mortgage loans is essential for home buyers as they navigate the home buying process. Realtors play a vital role in guiding buyers through the complexities of mortgage lending, explaining the various options, and helping them find the loan that best fits their financial goals and circumstances. By providing expertise and support throughout the loan selection process, realtors help buyers achieve their dream of homeownership with confidence and peace of mind.

Interest Rates, Terms, and Loan-to-Value Ratio

In the intricate world of real estate transactions, realtors play a pivotal role in guiding homebuyers through the complexities of the home purchasing process. Understanding key financial concepts like interest rates, loan terms, and loan-to-value (LTV) ratio is indispensable for realtors as they assist clients in making informed decisions and navigating the mortgage market effectively. In this section, we will delve into the nuances of interest rates, terms, and LTV ratio, highlighting their significance and practical implications for realtors when communicating with home buyers.

Interest Rates: Interest rates stand at the forefront of mortgage financing, exerting a profound influence on the affordability and feasibility of homeownership for buyers. As realtors engage with clients, conveying the dynamics of interest rates empowers buyers to comprehend the financial implications of their mortgage choices. Realtors should elucidate how fluctuations in interest rates impact monthly mortgage payments, total interest expenses, and long-term affordability.

When interest rates are low, realtors can emphasize the advantageous opportunity for buyers to lock in favorable rates, resulting in lower monthly payments and increased purchasing power. Conversely, during periods of rising interest rates, realtors can educate buyers about potential challenges, such as higher borrowing costs and reduced affordability. By providing insights into interest rate trends and forecasts, realtors empower buyers to make informed decisions aligned with their financial objectives and market conditions.

Loan Terms: Loan terms encompass the duration over which borrowers repay their mortgage loans, influencing monthly payments, interest expenses, and overall financial planning. Realtors play a crucial role in elucidating the implications of different loan terms to buyers, enabling them to make prudent choices tailored to their preferences and circumstances.

Realtors can educate buyers about the trade-offs between shorter and longer loan terms, highlighting how shorter terms offer the advantage of faster equity accumulation and lower total interest costs, albeit with higher monthly payments. Conversely, longer loan terms provide lower monthly payments but entail higher overall interest expenses over time. By facilitating discussions on loan terms, realtors empower buyers to weigh their options thoughtfully and select the term that aligns with their financial goals and lifestyle.

Loan-to-Value (LTV) Ratio: The loan-to-value (LTV) ratio serves as a crucial metric in mortgage lending, reflecting the relationship between the loan amount and the property's appraised value. Realtors can leverage their understanding of LTV ratio dynamics to help buyers comprehend the significance of equity and risk in the home buying process.

Educating buyers about LTV ratio implications enables realtors to illustrate the importance of building equity and minimizing risk exposure. A lower LTV ratio signifies a higher equity position for buyers, offering financial stability and favorable loan terms. Conversely, higher LTV ratios may entail additional costs, such as private mortgage insurance (PMI), and pose greater risk for buyers and lenders alike. By guiding buyers on strategies to optimize LTV ratios through down payments and property selection, realtors empower them to make informed decisions and navigate the mortgage landscape with confidence.

A comprehensive understanding of interest rates, loan terms, and loan-to-value ratio equips realtors with the knowledge and tools to effectively communicate with home buyers and facilitate successful real estate transactions. By demystifying financial concepts and empowering buyers to make informed decisions, realtors play a vital role in guiding clients toward achieving their homeownership dreams while navigating the intricacies of mortgage financing.

As we conclude Chapter 1, we recognize the critical role that effective communication and understanding of mortgage loans play in the real estate industry. Throughout this chapter, we've explored the fundamentals of mortgage loans, including key terms, documentation requirements, and different types of mortgage options available to homebuyers.

Realtors serve as educators, advocates, and facilitators in the homebuying process, guiding their clients through the complexities of mortgage lending and empowering them to make informed decisions. By leveraging their knowledge of mortgage loans, realtors help clients navigate the intricacies of financing their home purchase while addressing their concerns and facilitating seamless communication with lenders.

Chapter 2

The Best Lending Source for Your Client

In the rapidly evolving landscape of real estate finance, the role of a realtor extends far beyond the traditional confines of property transactions. As realtors, your professional responsibility encompasses a pivotal role: guiding your clients through the complex and often daunting journey of home financing. The essence of your advisory capacity lies in a deep-seated understanding of the myriad of lending options available, coupled with the acumen to match these options with the unique financial profiles and aspirations of your clients. This chapter is meticulously crafted to serve as an essential primer, designed to elevate your expertise and analytical prowess in navigating the multifaceted terrain of home financing options.

The architecture of home financing presents a spectrum of avenues, each with its distinct characteristics, advantages, and limitations. From the bedrock of traditional banks with their varied mortgage products and criteria to the strategic utility of mortgage brokers who provide access to an expansive network of lending solutions; from the community-centric credit unions offering tailored financial services to the agility of private lenders; the innovation-driven online lending platforms to the specialized government-backed loan programs, and the altruistic nonprofit organizations focusing on affordable homeownership solutions—each segment plays a critical role in the broader narrative of home buying and financing.

This comprehensive analysis is engineered to arm you, the realtor, with the requisite knowledge to adeptly advise your clients. By dissecting the nuances of each lending source, we aim to enhance your advisory toolkit, enabling you to offer bespoke financing guidance that aligns with the financial circumstances and homeownership dreams of your clients. The chapter delves into the operational mechanics, benefits, and potential drawbacks of traditional banks, mortgage brokers, credit unions, private lenders, online lenders, government-backed loan programs, nonprofit organizations, seller financing, and peer-to-peer lending. Our objective is to cultivate a sophisticated understanding of these diverse lending avenues, equipping you with the insights to navigate the complexities of home financing with confidence and competence.

As realtors, your role is integral to demystifying the home buying process for your clients, translating the technical jargon of finance into actionable strategies that pave the way to successful homeownership. This chapter is conceived as a strategic resource, intended to elevate your professional practice by enriching your financial literacy and advisory capabilities in the domain of home financing. Through a meticulous exploration of each lending avenue, we endeavor to empower you to guide your clients with precision, ensuring their journey towards homeownership is informed, strategic, and aligned with their long-term financial well-being. Welcome to a deep dive into the essential knowledge and strategies for navigating the complex landscape of home financing.

Traditional Banks

Traditional banks, as prominent fixtures in the realm of home financing, serve as primary sources for mortgage loans for many homebuyers. These institutions, typically characterized by their extensive physical presence and longstanding reputation, offer a diverse array of mortgage products tailored to meet various borrower needs. From conventional fixed-rate mortgages to adjustable-rate mortgages (ARMs) and government-backed loans such as FHA, VA, and USDA loans, traditional banks provide a comprehensive suite of lending options. As a realtor, possessing a deep understanding of the lending criteria and approval processes of different banks is paramount. This knowledge enables you to effectively guide your clients towards institutions that align with their financial goals and capabilities, ensuring they secure a mortgage that best suits their needs.

Pros:
1. **Wide Range of Loan Products:** Traditional banks offer a broad selection of mortgage products, catering to diverse borrower needs and preferences. This variety allows realtors to match clients with loan options that align with their financial circumstances and homeownership goals.

2. **Competitive Interest Rates:** Traditional banks often provide competitive interest rates on mortgage loans, leveraging their established presence and access to capital markets to offer favorable terms to borrowers.

3. **Established Reputation:** Banks with a long history and established reputation instill confidence in both borrowers and lenders. Clients may feel more secure obtaining a mortgage from a well-known bank, potentially streamlining the decision-making process and fostering trust in the lending institution.

4. **Physical Presence:** Traditional banks typically maintain a network of physical branches, offering clients the convenience of in-person banking services and access to knowledgeable staff who can provide personalized assistance throughout the mortgage application process.

Cons:
1. **Stringent Requirements:** Traditional banks may have stringent qualification criteria, including high credit score requirements, strict debt-to-income ratios, and sizable down payment expectations. Clients with less-than-perfect credit or limited financial resources may encounter challenges securing a mortgage through traditional banks.

2. **Limited Flexibility:** Banks adhere to established underwriting guidelines and lending policies, limiting their flexibility in accommodating unique borrower situations or unconventional financing scenarios. Clients with non-standard income sources or complex financial profiles may find it challenging to obtain loan approval from traditional banks.

3. **Lengthy Approval Process:** The mortgage approval process at traditional banks can be time-consuming, involving meticulous documentation review, thorough underwriting assessments, and multiple layers of approval. Delays in the approval process may frustrate clients seeking expedited loan processing or quick turnaround times.

4. **Less Personalized Service:** In the pursuit of efficiency and scalability, traditional banks may prioritize transaction volume over personalized customer service. Clients who value individualized attention and proactive communication throughout the mortgage process may feel underserved by the impersonal nature of bank interactions.

By thoroughly evaluating the pros and cons of traditional banks as mortgage lending sources, realtors can effectively guide their clients in navigating the complexities of home financing. Understanding the nuances of different banks' lending criteria, interest rates, and service offerings empowers realtors to advocate for their clients' best interests and facilitate successful mortgage transactions tailored to each client's unique needs and preferences.

Mortgage Brokers

Mortgage brokers play a pivotal role as intermediaries between borrowers and a multitude of lenders, facilitating access to a diverse range of loan products from various financial institutions. Collaborating with a mortgage broker affords clients the opportunity to explore exclusive deals and customized financing solutions that might not be readily accessible through traditional banks. From conventional mortgages to specialized programs catering to unique financial circumstances, mortgage brokers offer a comprehensive selection of lending options tailored to meet individual client needs.

Pros:
1. **Access to Diverse Loan Products:** Mortgage brokers provide clients with access to an extensive network of lenders, including banks, credit unions, and private lending institutions. This access expands the range of available loan products, allowing clients to explore options beyond what traditional banks may offer.

2. **Tailored Financing Solutions:** Mortgage brokers specialize in matching clients with loan products that align with their financial goals and circumstances. By assessing client needs and shopping around among different lenders, brokers can customize financing solutions to optimize terms, interest rates, and repayment structures.

3. **Negotiation Power:** Leveraging their industry expertise and established relationships with lenders, mortgage brokers have the ability to negotiate favorable terms on behalf of their clients. This negotiation power may result in lower interest rates, reduced fees, and more favorable loan terms, ultimately saving clients money over the life of the loan.

4. **Streamlined Application Process:** Mortgage brokers streamline the mortgage application process by handling paperwork, documentation, and communication with lenders on behalf of

their clients. This proactive approach minimizes administrative burden for clients and ensures efficient progress throughout the loan approval process.

Cons:

1. **Broker Fees:** Mortgage brokers typically charge fees for their services, which may include origination fees, broker commissions, or processing fees. These fees are often paid by the borrower and can add to the overall cost of obtaining a mortgage.

2. **Potential Conflicts of Interest:** While mortgage brokers are required to act in the best interests of their clients, there is a potential for conflicts of interest to arise. Brokers may receive commissions or incentives from lenders for placing loans with them, raising questions about the impartiality of their recommendations.

3. **Limited Direct Lender Access:** Some lenders may not work with mortgage brokers or offer exclusive deals only to borrowers who approach them directly. As a result, clients may miss out on certain loan products or incentives available through direct lender channels.

4. **Varied Broker Quality:** The quality of service and expertise among mortgage brokers can vary widely. While reputable brokers prioritize client satisfaction and compliance with industry standards, less experienced or unscrupulous brokers may engage in unethical practices or provide subpar service.

By carefully weighing the pros and cons of working with mortgage brokers, realtors can effectively guide their clients in selecting the most suitable home financing option for their individual needs. Educating clients about the role of mortgage brokers, their fee structures, and the potential benefits and drawbacks of broker-assisted mortgage transactions empowers them to make informed decisions that align with their long-term financial objectives.

Credit Unions

Credit unions represent member-owned financial cooperatives that operate under a cooperative structure, distinct from traditional banks or mortgage brokers. These institutions frequently offer competitive interest rates and personalized service to their members, catering to individuals seeking community-focused banking experiences. Although credit unions may impose more stringent membership criteria compared to conventional lenders, they can serve as an attractive lending option for clients who prioritize personalized financial services and community involvement. As a realtor, understanding the unique advantages and considerations associated with credit union membership enables you to effectively guide clients towards viable mortgage solutions that align with their preferences and financial goals.

Pros:
1. **Competitive Rates:** Credit unions often provide competitive interest rates on mortgage loans, leveraging their not-for-profit status and member-focused ethos to offer favorable terms to their members.

2. **Personalized Service:** Credit unions prioritize personalized service and member satisfaction, fostering strong relationships with borrowers and offering tailored financial solutions to meet individual needs.

3. **Community-Focused Banking:** Credit unions operate with a community-oriented mindset, reinvesting profits into member services, community development initiatives, and charitable endeavors, thereby contributing to the local economy and fostering a sense of belonging among members.

4. **Member Benefits:** Credit union membership may entail additional benefits beyond access to mortgage loans, such as lower fees, higher interest rates on savings accounts, and discounted financial products and services.

Cons:
1. **Membership Requirements:** Credit unions typically have membership requirements that may include residency within a specific geographic area, employment with certain organizations, or affiliation with particular groups or associations. These eligibility criteria may limit access to credit union membership for some clients.

2. **Limited Branch and ATM Network:** Compared to larger financial institutions, credit unions may have a more limited branch and ATM network, potentially posing challenges for

clients who prioritize convenience and accessibility in their banking relationships.

3. **Service Limitations:** Some credit unions may have limited service offerings or technological capabilities compared to larger banks, which could affect the range of mortgage products and services available to clients.

4. **Regulatory Constraints:** Credit unions are subject to regulatory oversight by federal and state authorities, which may impact their lending practices, risk management strategies, and operational flexibility.

By educating clients about the benefits and considerations of credit union membership, realtors can empower them to make informed decisions when exploring mortgage options. Assisting clients in navigating the credit union membership process and understanding the implications of joining a credit union enables realtors to enhance their clients' home buying experience and facilitate access to favorable mortgage solutions tailored to their unique financial preferences and circumstances.

Private Lenders

Private lenders represent a non-traditional option for home financing, involving individuals or private investment firms that extend loans directly to borrowers. Unlike traditional banks or credit unions, private lending arrangements typically offer greater flexibility in lending criteria and expedited approval processes. However, it's crucial for realtors to provide comprehensive guidance to their clients regarding the intricacies of private lending, enabling them to weigh the potential advantages and disadvantages and make informed decisions in line with their overarching financial objectives.

Pros:
1. **Flexibility in Lending Criteria:** Private lenders often have more flexible lending criteria compared to traditional financial institutions, allowing borrowers with non-standard financial profiles or unique circumstances to secure financing.

2. **Faster Approval Times:** Private lending transactions typically involve faster approval times and streamlined processes, enabling

borrowers to expedite the home buying process and capitalize on time-sensitive opportunities in the real estate market.

3. **Customized Loan Structures:** Private lenders can offer customized loan structures tailored to meet the specific needs and preferences of individual borrowers, including adjustable repayment terms, interest-only periods, and alternative collateral options.

4. **Access to Non-Conventional Financing:** Private lending provides access to non-conventional financing options that may not be available through traditional mortgage lenders, allowing borrowers to explore alternative routes to homeownership.

Cons:
1. **Higher Interest Rates:** Private lending arrangements often entail higher interest rates compared to traditional mortgage loans, resulting in increased long-term borrowing costs for borrowers.

2. **Limited Regulatory Oversight:** Private lenders may operate with limited regulatory oversight compared to traditional financial institutions, potentially exposing borrowers to greater risks related to lending practices, transparency, and consumer protection.

3. **Risk of Predatory Practices:** Some private lending entities may engage in predatory lending practices or impose unfavorable terms and conditions on borrowers, necessitating careful scrutiny and due diligence on the part of realtors and their clients.

4. **Lack of Consumer Protections:** Private lending transactions may lack the consumer protections and recourse mechanisms afforded by government-backed mortgage programs or traditional lending institutions, leaving borrowers vulnerable to unforeseen challenges or disputes.

By equipping yourself with a comprehensive understanding of the pros and cons of private lending, you can effectively guide your clients through the decision-making process and facilitate informed choices aligned with their long-term financial goals and risk tolerance levels. Additionally, realtors play a crucial role in mitigating potential risks associated with private lending by advocating for their clients' best interests, conducting thorough due diligence, and facilitating transparent communication between all parties involved in the transaction.

Online Lenders

Online lenders, propelled by the surge of financial technology (fintech), have emerged as prominent players in the mortgage lending landscape. Leveraging digital platforms, online lenders provide borrowers with streamlined application processes, competitive interest rates, and a suite of convenient online tools for managing every aspect of the loan process. For realtors, understanding the dynamics of online lending platforms is crucial in equipping clients with the knowledge needed to navigate the digital terrain effectively and make informed decisions regarding their mortgage options.

Pros:
1. **Streamlined Application Processes:** Online lenders offer simplified and user-friendly application processes, allowing borrowers to complete applications, upload documentation, and track the progress of their loan applications entirely online, minimizing paperwork and administrative hassles.

2. **Competitive Interest Rates:** Many online lenders boast competitive interest rates and fees, often rivaling or even surpassing those offered by traditional brick-and-mortar institutions. This competitive pricing can result in significant cost savings for borrowers over the life of their mortgage.

3. **Convenient Online Tools:** Online lenders provide borrowers with access to a comprehensive suite of digital tools and resources, including mortgage calculators, rate comparison tools, and online account management portals, empowering borrowers to make informed decisions and manage their loans efficiently.

4. **Accessibility and Convenience:** The digital nature of online lending platforms makes them accessible to borrowers from anywhere with an internet connection, offering unparalleled convenience and flexibility in the mortgage application and approval process.

Cons:
1. **Limited Personalized Service:** Online lenders may offer limited opportunities for personalized guidance and support compared to traditional lending institutions, potentially leaving some

borrowers feeling disconnected or underserved throughout the mortgage process.

2. **Risk of Cybersecurity Threats:** The reliance on digital platforms exposes borrowers to potential cybersecurity threats and data breaches, necessitating robust security measures and safeguards to protect sensitive personal and financial information.

3. **Varied Lending Standards:** Online lenders may have varied lending standards and criteria, making it essential for realtors to conduct thorough due diligence to ensure that clients meet the requirements of their chosen online lending platform.

4. **Potential for Impersonal Transactions:** The digital nature of online lending transactions can sometimes lead to impersonal interactions between borrowers and lenders, potentially resulting in a lack of clarity or miscommunication regarding loan terms and conditions.

By learning about the pros and cons of online lending, you can effectively guide your clients through the intricacies of the digital mortgage landscape, helping them leverage the benefits of online lending platforms while mitigating potential risks and challenges. Realtors play a pivotal role in facilitating transparent communication, conducting thorough due diligence, and advocating for their clients' best interests to ensure a seamless and successful online lending experience.

Government-Backed Loan Programs

Government-backed loan programs, including those administered by the Federal Housing Administration (FHA), the Department of Veterans Affairs (VA), and the United States Department of Agriculture (USDA), offer specialized financing solutions tailored to specific demographics, such as first-time homebuyers, veterans, and rural residents. Realtors serve as indispensable guides in navigating their clients through the intricacies of these government-sponsored loan programs, assisting them in understanding eligibility criteria, navigating the application process, and maximizing the benefits available.

Pros:

1. **Lower Down Payment Requirements:** Government-backed loan programs often feature lower down payment requirements compared to conventional loans, making homeownership more accessible to borrowers who may have limited funds for a down payment.

2. **Flexible Credit Requirements:** FHA loans, in particular, are known for their more lenient credit score requirements, allowing borrowers with less-than-perfect credit histories to qualify for financing. This flexibility expands homeownership opportunities for individuals with varying credit profiles.

3. **Competitive Interest Rates:** Government-backed loan programs typically offer competitive interest rates, ensuring that borrowers can secure financing at favorable terms, even if they have limited credit history or lower credit scores.

4. **Specialized Financing Options:** VA loans provide exclusive benefits to eligible veterans and service members, including no down payment requirements and the absence of private mortgage insurance (PMI), while USDA loans offer financing for homes in designated rural areas, promoting homeownership in underserved communities.

Cons:
1. **Property Eligibility Restrictions:** Government-backed loan programs often impose restrictions on the types of properties that qualify for financing, such as FHA's requirements for property condition and VA's appraisal standards. These restrictions may limit the pool of available homes for borrowers.

2. **Mortgage Insurance Premiums:** FHA loans require borrowers to pay mortgage insurance premiums (MIP) for the duration of the loan, increasing the overall cost of homeownership. Similarly, VA loans may require a funding fee, although this fee can often be financed into the loan amount.

3. **Documentation and Process Requirements:** Government-backed loan programs may have stricter documentation and process requirements compared to conventional loans, leading to potentially longer processing times and additional paperwork for borrowers and realtors alike.

4. **Limited Availability:** Some government-backed loan programs, such as VA and USDA loans, are only available to specific groups of borrowers, such as veterans or those purchasing homes in rural areas. This limited availability may exclude certain borrowers from accessing these financing options.

By equipping yourself with in-depth knowledge of the pros and cons of government-backed loan programs, they can effectively guide their clients in exploring these specialized financing options and making informed decisions that align with their homeownership goals and financial circumstances. Realtors' expertise in navigating the eligibility requirements and application process for government-sponsored loan programs is essential in facilitating a smooth and successful home buying experience for their clients.

Nonprofit Organizations

Realtors play a crucial role in guiding their clients through the complex landscape of home financing, including exploring alternative options such as nonprofit organizations and community development financial institutions (CDFIs). These entities offer affordable housing programs and down payment assistance initiatives aimed at assisting low- and moderate-income individuals and families in achieving homeownership. By collaborating with these organizations, realtors can connect their clients with valuable resources and support services that make the dream of homeownership more attainable and sustainable.

Pros:
1. **Affordable Housing Programs:** Nonprofit organizations and CDFIs often administer affordable housing programs designed to provide affordable mortgage options and down payment assistance to qualified borrowers. These programs can significantly lower the upfront costs associated with purchasing a home, making homeownership more accessible to individuals and families with limited financial resources.

2. **Down Payment Assistance:** Many nonprofit organizations offer down payment assistance programs to help homebuyers bridge the gap between their available funds and the required down payment amount. These assistance programs can take various forms, such as grants, forgivable loans, or deferred-payment

loans, providing borrowers with additional financial support to purchase a home.

3. **Educational Resources:** Nonprofit organizations and CDFIs typically offer educational resources and homeownership counseling services to empower homebuyers with the knowledge and skills needed to navigate the home buying process successfully. Realtors can leverage these resources to educate their clients about various aspects of homeownership, including budgeting, credit management, and mortgage options.

4. **Community Engagement:** Collaborating with nonprofit organizations and CDFIs allows realtors to engage with their local communities and support initiatives aimed at increasing homeownership opportunities for underserved populations. By actively participating in community development efforts, realtors can foster stronger relationships with community stakeholders and contribute to the overall well-being of their neighborhoods.

Cons:
1. **Limited Availability:** Affordable housing programs and down payment assistance initiatives offered by nonprofit organizations and CDFIs may have limited availability or eligibility requirements that restrict access to certain borrowers. Realtors need to carefully assess their clients' eligibility for these programs and explore alternative options if they do not qualify.

2. **Application Process:** The application process for affordable housing programs and down payment assistance initiatives may involve additional paperwork and documentation requirements compared to traditional mortgage financing. Realtors should be prepared to assist their clients in navigating the application process and meeting all necessary criteria.

3. **Income Restrictions:** Some affordable housing programs and down payment assistance initiatives have income restrictions that limit eligibility to low- and moderate-income households. Realtors need to verify their clients' income levels and ensure they meet the requirements of the programs they are interested in pursuing.

4. **Funding Constraints:** Nonprofit organizations and CDFIs may face funding constraints that impact the availability of affordable housing programs and down payment assistance initiatives.

Realtors should stay informed about funding opportunities and program changes to best serve their clients' needs.

By understanding the pros and cons of nonprofit organizations and CDFIs as alternative lending sources, realtors can effectively guide their clients in exploring these options and making informed decisions that align with their homeownership goals and financial circumstances. Collaborating with nonprofit organizations and CDFIs allows realtors to expand their network of resources and provide valuable support to clients seeking affordable and sustainable homeownership opportunities.

Seller Financing

Seller financing, also known as owner financing, presents an alternative option for homebuyers to secure financing directly from the seller rather than through a traditional mortgage lender. In this arrangement, the seller extends credit to the buyer by financing all or part of the purchase price of the home, allowing the buyer to make regular payments to the seller over an agreed-upon period. Realtors play a pivotal role in guiding their clients through the intricacies of seller financing agreements, ensuring transparency, fairness, and legal compliance throughout the process.

Pros:
1. **Flexibility in Terms:** Seller financing offers flexibility in negotiating terms such as the interest rate, repayment schedule, and down payment amount. This flexibility allows buyers and sellers to tailor the financing arrangement to meet their individual needs and preferences, potentially resulting in more favorable terms compared to traditional mortgage loans.

2. **Simplified Approval Process:** Seller financing eliminates the need for buyers to undergo the traditional mortgage approval process, which can be time-consuming and bureaucratic. Instead, buyers and sellers can negotiate directly on the terms of the financing agreement, streamlining the approval process and expediting the transaction.

3. **Accessible to Buyers with Limited Credit:** Seller financing may be accessible to buyers with limited credit history or less-than-perfect credit scores, as sellers have the discretion to

consider factors beyond conventional lending criteria when evaluating buyers' eligibility for financing.

4. **Potential Cost Savings:** Seller financing arrangements may offer cost savings for buyers in the form of reduced closing costs and origination fees typically associated with traditional mortgage loans. By bypassing the involvement of financial institutions, buyers can potentially save on upfront expenses related to loan origination and processing.

Cons:
1. **Higher Interest Rates:** Seller financing arrangements often come with higher interest rates compared to traditional mortgage loans, reflecting the increased risk assumed by sellers in extending credit directly to buyers. As a result, buyers may end up paying more in interest over the life of the loan compared to conventional financing options.

2. **Limited Seller Pool:** Not all sellers are willing or able to offer seller financing, limiting the pool of available properties for buyers seeking this type of financing. Buyers may need to conduct thorough market research and work closely with their realtors to identify sellers open to seller financing arrangements.

3. **Balloon Payments:** Seller financing agreements may include balloon payments, where a large lump sum is due at the end of the loan term. Buyers need to carefully consider their ability to make balloon payments and plan accordingly to avoid potential financial strain or default.

4. **Legal and Regulatory Considerations:** Seller financing agreements must comply with legal and regulatory requirements governing real estate transactions and lending practices. Realtors play a crucial role in ensuring that seller financing agreements adhere to applicable laws and regulations, protecting their clients from potential legal disputes or liabilities.

By understanding the pros and cons of seller financing, realtors can effectively advise their clients on whether this alternative financing option aligns with their financial goals and circumstances. Realtors should carefully evaluate the terms of seller financing agreements, negotiate on behalf of their clients, and facilitate a smooth and transparent transaction process to ensure a successful outcome for all parties involved.

Peer-to-Peer (P2P) Lending

Peer-to-peer (P2P) lending platforms have emerged as alternative sources of financing, allowing individuals to borrow money directly from investors or peers through online platforms. In P2P lending, borrowers create loan listings specifying their desired loan amount and interest rate, which potential investors can then fund either partially or in full. While P2P lending offers certain advantages such as flexibility and potentially competitive rates, it's crucial for homebuyers to thoroughly assess the terms and risks associated with these alternative lending arrangements. Realtors can play a vital role in educating their clients about the intricacies of P2P lending and guiding them in making well-informed decisions aligned with their financial objectives.

Pros:
1. **Accessibility:** P2P lending platforms provide an accessible alternative to traditional financial institutions, offering borrowers the opportunity to secure financing outside of the traditional banking system. This accessibility may benefit borrowers who have difficulty obtaining loans through conventional channels due to factors such as limited credit history or non-traditional income sources.

2. **Competitive Rates:** P2P lending platforms often boast competitive interest rates compared to traditional lenders, as they operate with lower overhead costs and may leverage technology to streamline the lending process. Borrowers with strong credit profiles may be able to access particularly favorable rates through P2P lending platforms, potentially saving on borrowing costs over time.

3. **Flexibility:** P2P lending arrangements may offer greater flexibility in loan terms and repayment options compared to traditional mortgage loans. Borrowers and investors can negotiate directly on factors such as loan duration, repayment schedule, and prepayment penalties, allowing for customized financing solutions tailored to individual needs and preferences.

4. **Diverse Investor Pool:** P2P lending platforms attract a diverse pool of investors seeking to earn returns on their investment capital. This diversity may translate to increased opportunities for

borrowers to secure funding, as investors may have varying risk appetites and investment criteria, resulting in a broader range of available loan options.

Cons:
1. **Risk of Default:** P2P lending carries inherent risks of borrower default, as there is no collateral securing the loan and investors bear the risk of loss if borrowers fail to repay. Economic downturns or unforeseen circumstances may increase the likelihood of borrower default, potentially impacting investors' returns and borrowers' creditworthiness.

2. **Limited Regulation:** P2P lending platforms may operate with less stringent regulatory oversight compared to traditional financial institutions, leading to potential gaps in consumer protection and risk management. Borrowers and investors should exercise caution when participating in P2P lending and conduct thorough due diligence on platform reputation, security measures, and regulatory compliance.

3. **Variable Loan Terms:** P2P lending platforms may offer variable loan terms and conditions, making it essential for borrowers to carefully review and understand the terms of the loan agreement before proceeding. Variability in loan terms such as interest rates, fees, and repayment schedules can impact the overall cost of borrowing and the borrower's ability to meet repayment obligations.

4. **Platform Reliability:** The reliability and stability of P2P lending platforms can vary, with some platforms experiencing operational challenges, funding delays, or platform failures. Borrowers and investors should research and assess the reputation and track record of P2P lending platforms to mitigate the risk of platform-related issues impacting their loan transactions.

Realtors play a crucial role in guiding their clients through the complexities of P2P lending, providing valuable insights and expertise to help them navigate this alternative financing option effectively. By educating their clients about the pros and cons of P2P lending, realtors empower them to make informed decisions aligned with their financial goals and circumstances, ultimately facilitating a successful home buying experience."

As we conclude this comprehensive journey through the multifaceted world of home financing options, it's imperative for you, the realtor, to recognize the critical role you play in your clients' home buying experiences. The detailed exploration of traditional banks, mortgage brokers, credit unions, private lenders, online lenders, government-backed loan programs, nonprofit organizations, seller financing, and peer-to-peer lending within this chapter is designed to significantly enhance your financial literacy and advisory capabilities. This knowledge is not merely academic; it is a practical toolkit that empowers you to guide your clients through the complexities of securing financing for their dream home with confidence and precision.

Your ability to navigate these diverse financing options and to provide tailored advice to your clients is what sets you apart in the competitive realm of real estate. Each financing avenue presents unique opportunities and challenges, and your expertise in assessing these, aligned with your clients' financial profiles and homeownership aspirations, is invaluable. By leveraging this knowledge, you can facilitate a smoother, more informed decision-making process, helping to align your clients' financial capabilities with their long-term goals.

The landscape of home financing is ever-evolving, with new products, regulations, and technologies continually emerging. Staying informed and adaptable is crucial in maintaining your edge as a trusted advisor. By fostering relationships with lenders, staying abreast of the latest trends and developments in real estate finance, and continuously educating both yourself and your clients, you can navigate this dynamic environment effectively.

In guiding your clients through their home financing choices, you do more than facilitate transactions; you build relationships, instill confidence, and contribute to the realization of their homeownership dreams. Your role is pivotal in transforming the complex process of home financing into a strategic, manageable journey towards successful homeownership.

This chapter, enriched with technical insights and devoid of metaphors, has been crafted to provide you with a solid foundation in the principles and practices of home financing. Use it as a reference, a guide, and a source of inspiration as you continue to serve your clients with the utmost professionalism and expertise. Remember, your guidance is a beacon that leads your clients through the intricacies of home financing, illuminating the path to homeownership with clarity, precision, and care.

Chapter 3

Preparing Clients for Mortgage Pre-Approval

In the pursuit of homeownership, mortgage pre-approval stands as a pivotal milestone, offering prospective buyers a tangible demonstration of their financial readiness and lending capacity. As real estate professionals, understanding the significance of mortgage pre-approval and its implications for home buyers is essential in guiding clients through the complexities of the real estate market.

Chapter 2 of our guide delves into the realm of mortgage pre-approval, exploring its multifaceted benefits and considerations for home buyers. From enhancing affordability and negotiating power to streamlining the buying process and demonstrating commitment, mortgage pre-approval serves as a catalyst for informed decision-making and successful real estate transactions.

In this chapter, we will dissect the criteria and considerations for mortgage pre-approval, providing insights into the key factors that influence the pre-approval process and highlighting how realtors can leverage this knowledge to empower their clients. From assessing financial stability and creditworthiness to navigating documentation requirements and property appraisals, we will unravel the intricacies of mortgage pre-approval, offering actionable guidance and resources for home buyers on their journey to homeownership.

Furthermore, we will explore actionable tips for improving credit score and financial readiness, recognizing the pivotal role that creditworthiness plays in the home buying process. By offering practical strategies and resources, realtors can empower clients to take control of their financial futures and overcome obstacles on the path to homeownership.

Ultimately, this chapter aims to equip realtors with the knowledge and tools to effectively guide clients through the mortgage pre-approval process, facilitating informed decision-making and empowering buyers to achieve their homeownership dreams with confidence and clarity. By leveraging our expertise and resources, we can navigate the complexities of mortgage pre-approval together, paving the way for seamless and rewarding real estate transactions for all parties involved.

Understanding Affordability: One of the primary advantages of seeking pre-approval is gaining a clear understanding of one's purchasing power and affordability. By undergoing a thorough financial assessment, including income verification, credit check, and debt-to-income ratio analysis, prospective buyers receive insights into the loan amount for which they qualify. This knowledge enables buyers to set realistic budgets, identify suitable properties within their price range, and avoid the disappointment of falling in love with homes beyond their financial means.

Strengthening Negotiating Power: Pre-approval not only empowers buyers with financial clarity but also enhances their negotiating leverage in competitive real estate markets. Sellers are more inclined to consider offers from pre-approved buyers, as it signals seriousness and financial readiness to proceed with the transaction. In multiple offer situations, pre-approval can tilt the scales in favor of the buyer, potentially securing a favorable deal or swaying the seller's decision in their favor.

Streamlining the Buying Process: Securing pre-approval streamlines the home buying process by expediting the mortgage approval process once an offer is made on a property. With pre-approval in hand, buyers can move quickly to finalize their financing arrangements, reducing the risk of delays or complications that could jeopardize the transaction. This efficiency not only enhances the buyer's experience but also instills confidence and trust among sellers and real estate agents, fostering smoother transactions and closing processes.

Identifying Potential Issues: Pre-approval serves as a proactive measure for buyers to address any potential issues or discrepancies in their financial profile before embarking on the home buying journey. By undergoing a thorough review of their credit history, income documentation, and financial assets, buyers can identify and rectify any errors, address outstanding debts, or take steps to improve their credit score if necessary. This preemptive approach minimizes the likelihood of encountering obstacles during the mortgage application process and ensures a smoother path to homeownership.

Demonstrating Seriousness and Commitment: Obtaining pre-approval demonstrates to sellers and real estate professionals that buyers are serious and committed to the home buying process. It signals readiness to proceed with the transaction and provides reassurance that the buyer has taken the necessary steps to secure financing. This confidence in the buyer's financial preparedness fosters trust and credibility, strengthening their position in negotiations and facilitating smoother interactions with sellers, agents, and other stakeholders involved in the transaction.

Pre-approval is a vital step in the home buying process, offering myriad benefits that extend beyond mere financial validation. From enhancing affordability and negotiating power to streamlining the buying process and demonstrating commitment, pre-approval provides buyers with invaluable insights and assurances that pave the way for successful and fulfilling homeownership experiences. As such, prospective home buyers should prioritize obtaining pre-approval early in their home buying journey to unlock its myriad benefits and set the stage for a seamless and rewarding real estate experience.

Pre-Approval: Criteria and Considerations for Buyers

Mortgage pre-approval stands as a crucial milestone in the home buying journey, offering buyers a tangible demonstration of their financial readiness and lending capacity. For realtors, understanding the criteria and considerations for mortgage pre-approval is essential in guiding clients through the intricacies of the real estate market. By leveraging this knowledge, realtors can effectively communicate with home buyers, provide tailored guidance, and facilitate informed decision-making. Now, we delve into the criteria for mortgage pre-approval, exploring the key factors that influence the pre-approval process and highlighting how realtors can use this information to empower their clients.

Financial Stability and Creditworthiness: At the core of mortgage pre-approval lies the assessment of an individual's financial stability and creditworthiness. Lenders evaluate various financial metrics, including credit score, income, employment history, and debt-to-income ratio, to gauge an applicant's ability to repay the loan. Realtors play a pivotal role in helping buyers understand the importance of maintaining healthy financial habits and building a strong credit profile. By educating clients on the significance of factors such as timely bill payments, debt management, and stable employment, realtors can empower buyers to present a compelling case for pre-approval and secure favorable loan terms.

Documentation and Verification: Mortgage pre-approval requires thorough documentation and verification of financial information to validate the accuracy and reliability of the applicant's financial profile. Realtors guide buyers through the process of assembling essential documents, such as pay stubs, tax returns, bank statements, and employment verification letters, ensuring completeness and accuracy. By proactively addressing potential documentation challenges and guiding buyers through the verification process, realtors streamline the pre-approval process, minimize delays, and enhance the likelihood of a successful outcome.

Property Appraisal and Valuation: In addition to assessing the borrower's financial credentials, mortgage pre-approval also entails an evaluation of the property's value and condition. Lenders conduct property appraisals to determine its market worth and ensure that it meets their lending criteria. Realtors collaborate with buyers to identify suitable properties that align with their budget, preferences, and financing options. By leveraging their local market expertise and network of industry contacts, realtors assist buyers in navigating the property appraisal process, negotiating favorable terms, and addressing any valuation discrepancies that may arise.

Mortgage Program Requirements: Different mortgage programs impose varying eligibility criteria and requirements for pre-approval, necessitating a tailored approach to the pre-approval process. Realtors familiarize themselves with the specific requirements of popular mortgage programs, such as FHA loans, VA loans, USDA loans, and conventional loans, to guide buyers towards the most suitable options. By aligning the buyer's financial profile with the eligibility criteria of different mortgage programs, realtors maximize their clients' chances of securing pre-approval and accessing favorable loan terms.

Communication and Collaboration: Effective communication and collaboration between realtors, buyers, and lenders are essential for navigating the pre-approval process successfully. Realtors serve as intermediaries, facilitating communication between buyers and lenders, clarifying expectations, and addressing any concerns or questions that may arise. By fostering open and transparent communication channels, realtors build trust, instill confidence, and ensure that the pre-approval process proceeds smoothly and efficiently.

Understanding the criteria for mortgage pre-approval is essential for both home buyers and realtors navigating the complexities of the real estate market. By familiarizing themselves with the financial stability and creditworthiness requirements, documentation and verification processes, property appraisal considerations, mortgage program requirements, and communication protocols involved in pre-approval, realtors can effectively guide their clients through the pre-approval process and empower them to make informed decisions. By leveraging their expertise and resources, realtors play a pivotal role in facilitating successful pre-approval outcomes, paving the way for seamless and rewarding real estate transactions for all parties involved.

Multiple Quotes from Different Lenders is Crucial

Encouraging clients to obtain multiple quotes from different lenders is crucial for ensuring they receive the best loan terms possible. Here's why realtors should emphasize this important step to their clients:

Comparison Shopping: Just like any other significant financial decision, comparing offers from multiple lenders allows homebuyers to explore a range of options and find the most favorable terms. Each lender may offer different interest rates, loan terms, and closing costs, so obtaining multiple quotes enables clients to make an informed decision based on their unique financial situation and preferences.

Access to Competitive Rates: Different lenders may have access to varying interest rates and loan programs. By shopping around, clients increase their chances of finding lenders offering competitive rates and terms, potentially saving them thousands of dollars over the life of the loan. Realtors can stress the importance of researching and comparing offers to ensure their clients secure the most favorable financing options available.

Negotiating Power: Armed with multiple quotes, clients gain negotiating leverage when discussing loan terms with lenders. Having alternative offers allows clients to advocate for better rates or terms, especially if they receive more favorable offers from competing lenders. Realtors can guide clients through the negotiation process, helping them articulate their preferences and secure the best possible deal.

Understanding Options: Obtaining multiple quotes provides clients with a comprehensive understanding of the mortgage market and available loan options. Clients may discover specialized loan programs or incentives offered by certain lenders that align with their needs and preferences. Realtors can help clients evaluate and compare the features of each loan offer, empowering them to make confident and well-informed decisions.

Protection Against Predatory Lending: By encouraging clients to shop around, realtors help safeguard against predatory lending practices. Clients who obtain multiple quotes are less likely to fall victim to inflated interest rates, excessive fees, or other unfavorable terms offered by unscrupulous lenders. Realtors play a vital role in advocating for their clients' best interests and ensuring they receive fair and transparent loan terms.

Mitigating Risk: Diversifying lender options reduces the risk of encountering delays or obstacles during the mortgage process. If one lender experiences processing delays or issues, clients have alternative options to pursue without compromising their homebuying timeline. Realtors can emphasize the importance of having backup plans in place to mitigate potential risks and uncertainties.

Personalized Recommendations: By reviewing multiple quotes, realtors can provide personalized recommendations tailored to their clients' specific needs and preferences. Realtors can leverage their expertise to analyze and compare loan offers, helping clients identify the most suitable financing options based on factors such as interest rates, loan terms, and closing costs. This personalized approach ensures that clients receive financing solutions aligned with their financial goals and circumstances.

Encouraging clients to obtain multiple quotes from different lenders is essential for securing the best possible loan terms and ensuring a successful homebuying experience. Realtors play a crucial role in guiding clients through the mortgage shopping process, empowering them to make informed decisions and achieve their homeownership goals with confidence and peace of mind.

Tips for Improving Credit Score

In the realm of real estate, achieving homeownership hinges significantly on a buyer's creditworthiness and financial readiness. Aspiring home buyers often grapple with the challenge of navigating the complexities of credit scoring and financial management. Realtors play a crucial role in guiding clients through this process, offering invaluable advice and resources to enhance their credit score and financial preparedness. We are going to explore actionable tips for improving credit score and financial readiness, highlighting how realtors can leverage this information to empower their clients on the path to homeownership.

Understand Credit Score Components: To improve their credit score, clients must first understand the factors that influence it. Key components include payment history, credit utilization, length of credit history, new credit inquiries, and credit mix. Realtors can educate clients on the significance of each component and provide guidance on how to prioritize efforts for maximum impact.

Review Credit Reports Regularly: Encourage clients to obtain copies of their credit reports from major credit bureaus and review them for inaccuracies or discrepancies. Realtors can recommend reputable credit monitoring services and guide clients through the process of disputing errors to ensure their credit reports accurately reflect their financial history.

Establish Good Payment Habits: Timely payment of bills, loans, and credit card balances is essential for maintaining a positive credit score. Realtors can advise clients to set up automatic payments or reminders to avoid missing due dates and negatively impacting their creditworthiness. Emphasize the importance of consistency and reliability in payment habits.

Manage Debt Wisely: High levels of debt relative to income can adversely affect credit scores and financial stability. Realtors can counsel clients on strategies for managing debt responsibly, such as paying down existing balances, avoiding excessive use of credit cards, and refraining from opening new accounts unnecessarily. Encourage clients to prioritize debt repayment and explore debt consolidation options if feasible.

Keep Credit Utilization Low: Credit utilization, or the ratio of credit card balances to credit limits, is a significant factor in credit scoring. Recommend that clients aim to keep their credit utilization below 30% to demonstrate responsible credit management. Realtors can suggest strategies such as paying down balances, requesting credit limit increases, or spreading out spending across multiple cards to lower utilization ratios.

Build Positive Credit History: Encourage clients to diversify their credit mix by maintaining a mix of installment loans and revolving credit accounts. Realtors can advise clients to consider opening a secured credit card or becoming an authorized user on a family member's account to establish or rebuild credit history. Emphasize the importance of patience and persistence in building a positive credit profile over time.

Seek Professional Guidance: For clients facing complex credit challenges or struggling to improve their credit score independently, seeking professional guidance from credit counselors or financial advisors may be beneficial. Realtors can provide referrals to reputable professionals and offer ongoing support and encouragement throughout the credit improvement process.

Empowering home buyers to improve their credit score and financial readiness is essential for achieving the dream of homeownership. Realtors serve as trusted advisors and advocates, guiding clients through the intricacies of credit scoring and financial management with expertise and empathy. By offering actionable tips, resources, and support, realtors empower their clients to take control of their financial futures and embark on the journey to homeownership with confidence and clarity. By leveraging their knowledge and resources, realtors play a pivotal role in helping clients overcome obstacles and realize their homeownership goals.

★

Chapter 3 of our comprehensive guide has equipped both real estate professionals and home buyers with invaluable insights into the realm of mortgage pre-approval. As we conclude this chapter, let's recap the key takeaways and reflect on the importance of preparing clients for this crucial step in the home buying journey.

Mortgage pre-approval serves as a pivotal milestone, offering prospective buyers a tangible demonstration of their financial readiness and lending capacity. It provides buyers with essential insights into their purchasing power, affordability, and negotiating leverage in the real estate market. By undergoing a thorough financial assessment, including income verification, credit check, and debt-to-income ratio analysis, buyers can set realistic budgets, identify suitable properties, and streamline the buying process.

Throughout this chapter, we've explored the multifaceted benefits of mortgage pre-approval, ranging from enhancing affordability and negotiating power to identifying potential issues and demonstrating commitment. We've also delved into the criteria and considerations for mortgage pre-approval, highlighting the importance of financial stability, documentation, property appraisal, mortgage program requirements, and effective communication.

Furthermore, we've discussed the significance of encouraging clients to obtain multiple quotes from different lenders, emphasizing the importance of comparison shopping, access to competitive rates, negotiating power, understanding options, protection against predatory lending, mitigating risk, and personalized recommendations.

Lastly, we've provided actionable tips for improving credit score and financial readiness, recognizing the pivotal role that creditworthiness plays in the home buying process. By offering practical strategies and resources, realtors can empower clients to take control of their financial futures and overcome obstacles on the path to homeownership.

As we move forward in the home buying journey, it's essential for real estate professionals to leverage their expertise and resources to guide clients through the complexities of mortgage pre-approval with confidence and clarity. By prioritizing preparation and empowering clients to make informed decisions, we can pave the way for successful and fulfilling real estate transactions for all parties involved.

Chapter 4

Understanding Mortgage Documentation

In this chapter, we delve into the intricacies of the documentation required for mortgage applications, shedding light on the essential paperwork that home buyers need to navigate in their journey to homeownership.

Securing a mortgage is a significant milestone in the home buying process, and it entails a thorough review of various financial documents by lenders. From identification and personal information to proof of income, asset documentation, employment verification, credit history, and property-related documents, the mortgage application process demands meticulous attention to detail and compliance with lender requirements.

Realtors play a pivotal role in educating and guiding home buyers through the documentation process, ensuring accuracy, completeness, and timeliness in the submission of required paperwork. By providing clarity, support, and expert guidance, realtors empower home buyers to navigate the complexities of mortgage documentation with confidence and ease, ultimately helping them achieve their homeownership goals.

Throughout this chapter, we will explore the key components of mortgage documentation, highlighting their significance in the approval process and offering insights into how realtors can effectively communicate this information to home buyers. We will also discuss the importance of accurate and timely documentation submission, emphasizing its role in establishing credibility, facilitating the underwriting process, avoiding rejections and delays, building trust and confidence, and meeting closing targets.

Additionally, we will address common pitfalls to avoid during the documentation process, such as providing incomplete or inaccurate information, missing deadlines, failing to provide required documentation, ignoring requests for additional information, and lacking communication with lenders. By identifying these potential pitfalls and offering practical strategies for overcoming them, we aim to empower home buyers to navigate the documentation process successfully and achieve their homeownership dreams with confidence and peace of mind.

Join us as we embark on a journey into the realm of mortgage documentation, exploring its intricacies, challenges, and opportunities for success. With the guidance and expertise of realtors, home buyers can navigate the documentation process with clarity and ease, paving the way for a seamless and rewarding homeownership experience.

1. **Identification and Personal Information:** One of the fundamental requirements for a mortgage application is providing identification and personal information. This includes government-issued identification such as a driver's license or passport, as well as Social Security numbers for all applicants. Realtors can stress the importance of accuracy and completeness in providing this information to avoid delays in the application process.

2. **Proof of Income:** Lenders typically require documentation of income to assess a borrower's ability to repay the mortgage. This may include recent pay stubs, W-2 forms, or tax returns for self-employed individuals. Realtors can advise home buyers to gather these documents in advance and to be prepared to provide additional documentation if income sources are varied or complex.

3. **Asset Documentation:** Lenders also require documentation of assets to verify the source of funds for the down payment and closing costs. This may include bank statements, investment account statements, and retirement account statements. Realtors can educate home buyers on the importance of transparency and consistency in asset documentation to avoid potential red flags during the underwriting process.

4. **Employment Verification:** Lenders typically verify employment to ensure borrowers have stable income sources. This may involve providing recent pay stubs, employment verification forms, or contact information for employers. Realtors can guide home buyers on the proper procedures for obtaining and submitting employment verification documents and emphasize the importance of timely communication with employers if needed.

5. **Credit History:** Lenders assess borrowers' creditworthiness by reviewing their credit history and scores. Home buyers must authorize lenders to access their credit reports, which provide details of their credit accounts, payment history, and outstanding debts. Realtors can explain the significance of maintaining good credit and offer guidance on steps home buyers can take to improve their credit profiles if needed.

6. **Property Documentation:** In addition to borrower-related documents, mortgage applications also require documentation related to the property being purchased. This may include a purchase agreement, property appraisal, and homeowners insurance information. Realtors can assist home buyers in obtaining and organizing these documents to ensure a smooth transaction process.

Understanding the required documents for mortgage applications is essential for home buyers embarking on the journey to homeownership. Realtors play a vital role in educating and guiding home buyers through the documentation process, ensuring compliance with lender requirements and facilitating a seamless transaction experience. By providing clarity, support, and expert guidance, realtors empower home buyers to navigate the complexities of mortgage applications with confidence and ease, ultimately helping them achieve their homeownership goals.

Accurate and Timely Documentation in Mortgage Applications

In the realm of real estate transactions, accuracy and timeliness are paramount, especially when it comes to submitting documentation for mortgage applications. The process of securing a mortgage involves a meticulous review of various financial documents by lenders, and any discrepancies or delays in documentation submission can significantly impact the outcome of the application. In this section, as we navigate into the importance of accurate and timely documentation submission in mortgage applications, with a focus on how realtors can effectively communicate this information to home buyers.

Establishing Credibility: Accurate and timely documentation submission is crucial for establishing credibility with lenders. Realtors can emphasize to home buyers that presenting complete and error-free documentation reflects positively on their financial responsibility and reliability as borrowers. This, in turn, enhances their chances of approval and favorable loan terms.

Facilitating the Underwriting Process: Lenders rely heavily on the documentation provided by borrowers to assess their creditworthiness and ability to repay the mortgage. Any inaccuracies or missing information can prolong the underwriting process and lead to unnecessary delays in loan approval. Realtors can stress the importance of thoroughness and attention to detail in documentation submission to streamline the underwriting process and expedite loan approval.

Avoiding Rejections and Delays: Inaccurate or incomplete documentation is one of the primary reasons for mortgage application rejections or delays. Realtors can educate home buyers on the potential consequences of inadequate documentation, including the risk of losing out on their desired property or facing higher interest rates due to extended processing times. By ensuring accurate and timely submission of documents, realtors help mitigate these risks and keep the transaction on track.

Building Trust and Confidence: Timely submission of documentation demonstrates a proactive and organized approach to the mortgage application process, which can instill trust and confidence in lenders. Realtors can convey to home buyers that prompt and thorough documentation submission signals their commitment to the transaction and enhances their credibility as serious buyers. This, in turn, fosters positive relationships with lenders and strengthens the overall transaction experience.

Meeting Deadlines and Closing Targets: Accurate and timely documentation submission is essential for meeting closing deadlines and targets. Delays in documentation processing can disrupt the entire transaction timeline, leading to missed closing dates and additional costs for both buyers and sellers. Realtors can stress the importance of adhering to documentation deadlines and proactively addressing any issues that may arise to ensure a smooth and timely closing process.

Accurate and timely documentation submission is a critical aspect of the mortgage application process that cannot be overstated. Realtors play a pivotal role in guiding home buyers through this process, emphasizing the importance of thoroughness, accuracy, and timeliness in documentation submission. By ensuring that borrowers provide complete and error-free documentation, realtors help expedite the underwriting process, mitigate risks of rejection or delays, and ultimately facilitate successful and timely closings. With clear communication and diligent oversight, realtors empower home buyers to navigate the complexities of documentation submission with confidence and ease, paving the way for a seamless and rewarding homeownership journey.

Navigating the Documentation Process

The documentation process is a crucial aspect of securing a mortgage, yet it can be fraught with pitfalls that may derail the home buying journey if not navigated carefully. Moving on, we explore some common pitfalls to avoid during the documentation process, with a focus on how realtors can empower home buyers to sidestep these obstacles and achieve their homeownership goals with confidence.

Incomplete or Inaccurate Information: One of the most common pitfalls in the documentation process is providing incomplete or inaccurate information to lenders. Realtors can stress the importance of double-checking all documentation for accuracy and ensuring that no crucial information is omitted. Emphasizing the need for thoroughness and attention to detail can help home buyers avoid delays and potential rejections due to incomplete or inaccurate documentation.

Missing Deadlines: Missing deadlines for documentation submission can significantly disrupt the mortgage application process and delay the closing of the transaction. Realtors can educate home buyers on the importance of adhering to all deadlines set by lenders and ensuring that all required documents are submitted in a timely manner. Implementing a system of reminders and follow-ups can help home buyers stay organized and on track with documentation deadlines.

Failure to Provide Required Documentation: Lenders have specific requirements for the documentation needed to process a mortgage application, and failure to provide all required documents can lead to delays or rejections. Realtors can work closely with home buyers to ensure that they understand exactly what documents are needed and help them gather and submit the necessary paperwork promptly. Providing a checklist of required documents can help streamline the process and prevent oversights.

Ignoring Requests for Additional Information: During the underwriting process, lenders may request additional information or documentation to clarify certain aspects of the borrower's financial situation. Ignoring or delaying responses to these requests can prolong the processing time and create unnecessary complications. Realtors can advise home buyers to promptly respond to any requests for additional information and assist them in gathering and submitting the required documentation in a timely manner.

Lack of Communication with Lenders: Effective communication with lenders is essential throughout the documentation process to address any questions or concerns that may arise and ensure a smooth and timely approval process. Realtors can encourage home buyers to maintain open lines of communication with their lenders and promptly respond to any inquiries or requests for information. Acting as a liaison between home buyers and lenders, realtors can facilitate clear and timely communication to keep the documentation process on track.

Navigating the documentation process successfully requires vigilance, attention to detail, and proactive communication. By avoiding common pitfalls such as providing incomplete or inaccurate information, missing deadlines, failing to provide required documentation, ignoring requests for additional information, and lacking communication with lenders, home buyers can streamline the mortgage application process and enhance their chances of approval. Realtors play a crucial role in guiding home buyers through this process, providing support, guidance, and expertise to help them navigate the complexities of documentation submission with confidence and ease. With careful planning, diligence, and collaboration, home buyers can overcome potential pitfalls and achieve their homeownership dreams with success.

Navigating the Mortgage Application Process

Welcome to Chapter 5, where we embark on a comprehensive exploration of the intricate journey involved in securing a mortgage, a cornerstone of the home buying process. In this chapter, we delve into the labyrinth of steps that constitute the mortgage application process, demystifying each stage to equip both real estate professionals and prospective homeowners with the knowledge and confidence needed to navigate this terrain successfully.

The mortgage application process, often perceived as a daunting endeavor, is illuminated through a detailed step-by-step guide, offering clarity and empowerment to those embarking on the path to homeownership. With a primary focus on the pivotal role of realtors, we unravel the intricacies of each stage, emphasizing their instrumental support in guiding home buyers through the labyrinth of paperwork, negotiations, and approvals.

Our journey commences with pre-application preparation, where prospective buyers lay the groundwork for their mortgage endeavor by meticulously organizing financial documents and evaluating their creditworthiness. Realtors assume the role of advisors, steering buyers towards proactive measures to enhance their financial standing and streamline the application process.

Next, we delve into the critical phase of pre-approval, illuminating its significance as the initial stamp of eligibility conferred by a lender. Realtors emerge as facilitators, aiding buyers in navigating the pre-approval process and leveraging their newfound borrowing capacity to advance confidently in the pursuit of their dream home.

As the narrative progresses, we explore the pivotal juncture of property selection and offer submission, underscoring the indispensable role of realtors in advocating for buyers' interests and orchestrating seamless negotiations with sellers. With a keen eye for market dynamics and a deft hand in crafting compelling offers, realtors navigate this phase with finesse, ensuring that buyers' aspirations align harmoniously with market realities.

The formal mortgage application stage unfolds as buyers transition from aspiration to action, submitting comprehensive documentation to their chosen lender under the guidance of their realtor. Clear communication and meticulous attention to detail emerge as linchpins in this phase, fostering a collaborative environment conducive to swift and efficient processing.

Our narrative reaches its zenith with underwriting and approval, where the intricate dance between borrower, lender, and realtor culminates in the final verdict on loan viability. Realtors emerge as steadfast advocates, navigating potential obstacles and fostering transparent communication to expedite the approval process and safeguard buyers' interests.

The journey does not conclude with approval but extends into the realms of home appraisal, inspection, closing preparation, and post-closing follow-up. At each juncture, realtors stand as pillars of support, orchestrating seamless transitions and ensuring that buyers' visions of homeownership materialize with clarity, confidence, and peace of mind.

As we traverse the landscape of the mortgage application process, clarity emerges from complexity, and empowerment blossoms from understanding. With realtors as trusted guides, home buyers embark on a transformative journey, navigating the labyrinth of mortgage lending with resilience, resolve, and the unwavering assurance of a brighter tomorrow.

Demystifying the Mortgage Application Process

The mortgage application process can seem daunting for many home buyers, but understanding each step can help demystify the process and empower buyers to navigate it with confidence. I'm going to provide a detailed step-by-step guide to the mortgage application process, with an emphasis on how realtors can use this information to support and guide home buyers through every stage of the journey.

Pre-Application Preparation: Before diving into the mortgage application process, home buyers should take time to prepare their financial documents and assess their creditworthiness. Realtors can advise buyers to gather essential documents such as pay stubs, tax returns, bank statements, and proof of assets. Additionally, realtors can recommend that buyers check their credit reports for any errors and take steps to improve their credit score if necessary.

Pre-Approval: The first official step in the mortgage application process is obtaining pre-approval from a lender. Realtors can help buyers find reputable lenders and assist them in completing the pre-approval application. Pre-approval provides buyers with a clear understanding of their borrowing capacity and strengthens their position when making offers on properties.

Property Selection and Offer: Once pre-approved, home buyers work with their realtors to find their dream home and make an offer. Realtors play a crucial role in negotiating with sellers and guiding buyers through the offer process, ensuring that their interests are protected and their offers are competitive.

Formal Mortgage Application: After an offer is accepted, buyers submit a formal mortgage application to their chosen lender. Realtors can help buyers complete the application accurately and ensure that all required documentation is submitted promptly. Clear communication between realtors, buyers, and lenders is essential at this stage to keep the process moving smoothly.

Underwriting and Approval: Once the mortgage application is submitted, the lender conducts underwriting to assess the buyer's creditworthiness and the property's value. Realtors can provide support to buyers during this stage by addressing any concerns raised by the lender and facilitating communication between all parties involved. Buyers may need to provide additional documentation or clarification during underwriting, and realtors can help streamline this process.

Home Appraisal and Inspection: As part of the mortgage application process, the lender typically requires a home appraisal to determine the property's value and ensure it meets lending standards. Realtors can assist buyers in scheduling a home inspection to identify any potential issues or defects that may affect the property's value or the buyer's decision to proceed with the purchase.

Closing Preparation: As the closing date approaches, realtors play a vital role in coordinating with all parties involved, including lenders, attorneys, and title companies, to ensure a smooth and successful closing. Realtors can help buyers review closing documents, understand their obligations, and address any last-minute issues that may arise.

The mortgage application process is a complex yet manageable journey that requires careful planning, preparation, and collaboration. By following a step-by-step guide and leveraging the expertise and support of their realtors, home buyers can navigate the process with confidence and achieve their homeownership dreams. Realtors play a pivotal role in guiding buyers through each stage of the process, providing invaluable support, advice, and advocacy to ensure a seamless and successful transaction. With a clear understanding of the mortgage application process and the guidance of a trusted realtor, home buyers can embark on their homeownership journey with clarity, confidence, and peace of mind.

Understanding the Roles of Loan Officers and Underwriters

In the intricate landscape of mortgage lending, two key players hold significant sway: the loan officer and the underwriter. Understanding their respective roles and how they intersect is crucial for both home buyers and realtors navigating the mortgage process. Let's head into into the roles of loan officers and underwriters, with an emphasis on how realtors can leverage this knowledge to support and guide home buyers effectively.

The Role of the Loan Officer: Loan officers serve as the primary point of contact between borrowers and lenders throughout the mortgage application process. Their responsibilities include:

- **Assessing Borrower Eligibility:** Loan officers review borrowers' financial documents, credit history, and employment information to determine their eligibility for various loan programs.

- **Providing Guidance and Advice:** Loan officers offer personalized guidance and advice to help borrowers understand their mortgage options, choose the right loan product, and navigate the application process.

- **Facilitating the Application Process:** Loan officers assist borrowers in completing loan applications, collecting required documentation, and submitting the application to the lender.

- **Communicating with Borrowers:** Loan officers keep borrowers informed about the status of their application, address any concerns or questions they may have, and provide updates throughout the process.

The Role of the Underwriter: Underwriters play a critical behind-the-scenes role in the mortgage approval process. Their responsibilities include:

- **Assessing Risk:** Underwriters evaluate borrowers' financial profiles, creditworthiness, and the property being financed to assess the level of risk associated with approving the loan.

- **Reviewing Documentation:** Underwriters meticulously review borrowers' financial documentation, including income statements, tax returns, and bank statements, to ensure accuracy and compliance with lending guidelines.

- **Making Lending Decisions:** Based on their assessment of risk and adherence to lending criteria, underwriters make the final decision on whether to approve, deny, or conditionally approve a mortgage application.

- **Mitigating Risk:** Underwriters identify potential red flags or discrepancies in borrowers' financial profiles and take steps to mitigate risk by requiring additional documentation or conditions before finalizing the loan approval.

How Realtors Can Support Home Buyers: Realtors play a pivotal role in guiding home buyers through the mortgage process and can leverage their understanding of loan officers and underwriters to provide valuable support:

- **Educating Buyers:** Realtors can educate buyers about the roles of loan officers and underwriters, helping them understand the importance of timely communication, accurate documentation, and cooperation throughout the process.

- **Facilitating Communication:** Realtors act as liaisons between home buyers and loan officers, ensuring clear and effective communication and addressing any questions or concerns that may arise.

- **Managing Expectations:** Realtors can help manage buyers' expectations by explaining the timeline and potential challenges of the mortgage approval process, fostering realistic expectations and reducing stress.

- **Advocating for Buyers:** Realtors advocate for their clients' best interests by working closely with loan officers and underwriters to address any issues or obstacles that may arise during the application process, advocating for timely resolution and favorable outcomes.

Loan officers and underwriters play integral roles in the mortgage process, working together to assess borrower eligibility, mitigate risk, and facilitate loan approval. Realtors can empower home buyers by providing guidance, support, and advocacy throughout the process, leveraging their understanding of the roles of loan officers and underwriters to navigate challenges and achieve successful outcomes. By fostering clear communication, managing expectations, and advocating for their clients' best interests, realtors can help home buyers navigate the complex landscape of mortgage lending with confidence and peace of mind.

Timeline from Application to Closing

Embarking on the journey of homeownership involves navigating a series of milestones from mortgage application to closing. Understanding the timeline and key milestones of this process is essential for both home buyers and realtors. We are going to discuss the timeline and key milestones of the mortgage process, with an emphasis on how realtors can use this information to guide and support home buyers effectively.

1. **Pre-Application Phase:**

   - Exploring Financing Options: Before formally applying for a mortgage, home buyers work with their realtor to explore various financing options, determine their budget, and assess their eligibility for different loan programs.

   - Pre-Approval: Home buyers obtain pre-approval from a lender, which involves submitting financial documentation and undergoing a credit check to determine the maximum loan amount they qualify for.

2. **Mortgage Application:**

   - Submission of Application: Once home buyers find a property and have an accepted offer, they submit a formal mortgage application to their chosen lender.

   - Documentation Collection: Home buyers work closely with their realtor to gather and submit required documentation, including income statements, tax returns, and bank statements, to support their loan application.

   - Underwriting Process: The lender's underwriter reviews the application and supporting documentation to assess the borrower's creditworthiness and the property's eligibility for financing.

3. **Loan Approval and Processing:**

- Conditional Loan Approval: If the underwriter approves the loan application, they may issue a conditional loan approval, outlining any additional documentation or requirements needed to finalize the loan.

- Property Appraisal: The lender orders an appraisal to determine the fair market value of the property and ensure it meets lending criteria.

- Title Search and Insurance: The title company conducts a title search to verify ownership of the property and purchase title insurance to protect against any defects or claims on the property's title.

4. **Closing Preparation:**

- Clearing Conditions: Home buyers work with their realtor to address any outstanding conditions or requirements outlined in the conditional loan approval.

- Closing Disclosure: The lender provides the home buyers with a closing disclosure, detailing the final terms of the loan, including interest rate, closing costs, and monthly payments.

5. **Closing:**

- Final Walkthrough: Home buyers conduct a final walkthrough of the property to ensure it is in the agreed-upon condition and any negotiated repairs have been completed.

- Signing Documents: Home buyers attend the closing meeting, where they sign the final loan documents and transfer ownership of the property.

- Funding and Recording: Once all documents are signed and funds are transferred, the lender disburses the loan funds, and the transaction is recorded with the appropriate county office.

6. **Post-Closing:**

- **Homeownership:** Home buyers officially take possession of the property and begin the process of homeownership, including moving in and setting up utilities.
- **Follow-Up:** Realtors follow up with home buyers to ensure a smooth transition into their new home and address any questions or concerns that may arise post-closing.

Navigating the mortgage process from application to closing involves a series of key milestones, each with its own timeline and requirements. By understanding these milestones and guiding home buyers through each step, realtors can play a pivotal role in ensuring a seamless and successful home buying experience. From pre-application planning to post-closing follow-up, realtors provide invaluable support and expertise, helping home buyers navigate the complex landscape of mortgage lending with confidence and peace of mind.

As we wrap up Chapter 5, "Navigating the Mortgage Application Process," it's crucial to underscore the importance of the comprehensive insights and detailed guidance provided throughout this exploration. This chapter serves not only as a roadmap for real estate professionals in guiding their clients through the mortgage application process but also as a foundational pillar enhancing their advisory role in the home buying journey. By dissecting each phase of the mortgage application, from pre-application preparation to the closing stages, we've endeavored to arm you, the realtor, with the knowledge and tools necessary to navigate this complex process effectively.

Understanding the sequential steps—beginning with the critical pre-application preparations, moving through the intricacies of obtaining pre-approval, selecting the property, formalizing the mortgage application, and culminating in the underwriting and approval stages—empowers you to provide nuanced advice and support to your clients. This chapter emphasizes the pivotal role of realtors in managing expectations, facilitating communication between all parties, and advocating for the buyer's interests throughout the mortgage application process.

Moreover, the exploration into the roles of loan officers and underwriters illuminates the operational mechanics behind mortgage lending, enabling you to guide your clients with an informed perspective. By fostering a collaborative relationship with these key figures, you enhance the efficiency and effectiveness of the process, ensuring that your clients' experiences are as smooth and stress-free as possible.

The journey from the initial application to the final closing involves a series of critical milestones. By mastering the timelines and requirements outlined in this chapter, you position yourself as an indispensable resource to your clients, adept at steering them through each stage with confidence and expertise. Your role transcends mere transactional assistance; you become a trusted advisor, a facilitator of dreams, and a key player in the realization of homeownership aspirations.

In summary, Chapter 5 equips you with a deep understanding of the mortgage application process, enabling you to guide your clients through every step with confidence. Your ability to demystify this complex process, combined with your commitment to advocating for your clients' best interests, not only enhances their home buying experience but also solidifies your reputation as a knowledgeable and reliable real estate professional. As the real estate landscape continues to evolve, let the insights and strategies detailed in this chapter serve as your compass, guiding your professional practice towards excellence in service and success in facilitating homeownership.

Chapter 6

Mortgage Loan Programs and Options

In our earlier discussion in Chapter 1, we embarked on an exploration of the multifaceted landscape of mortgage loans. This intricate domain spans a wide spectrum, featuring a plethora of options tailored to accommodate diverse financial circumstances and preferences. From the stalwart stability of conventional 30-year fixed-rate mortgages to the nuanced flexibility of alternative documentation loans and the specialized focus of CDFI loans, the array of choices can seem daunting at first glance.

However, fear not, for this chapter serves as a guiding beacon, illuminating the intricacies of each loan type with meticulous detail. Here, we embark on an in-depth journey, peeling back the layers to reveal the essence of each loan, its inherent strengths, weaknesses, and the unique scenarios in which it shines brightest.

By the time we conclude our exploration, you'll possess a comprehensive understanding of the diverse tapestry of mortgage loans, equipped with the knowledge to navigate this complex terrain with confidence and clarity. So, let's dive in and unravel the mysteries of mortgage lending together, empowering you to make informed decisions that align perfectly with your unique needs and aspirations.

Loan Programs and Options

Conventional Loans

Description: Conventional loans are mortgage loans that are not backed by the government. They are typically offered by private lenders and follow guidelines set by Fannie Mae and Freddie Mac, two government-sponsored enterprises. Conventional loans often require higher credit scores and down payments compared to government-backed loans.

Pros:
1. **Flexibility:** Conventional loans offer flexibility in terms of loan amounts, repayment terms, and property types.

2. **No Upfront Mortgage Insurance:** Unlike FHA loans, conventional loans do not require upfront mortgage insurance premiums, potentially reducing overall loan costs.

3. **Lower Costs with High Credit Scores:** Borrowers with excellent credit scores may qualify for lower interest rates and fees compared to other loan types.

Cons:
1. **Stricter Requirements:** Conventional loans typically have stricter qualification criteria regarding credit scores, debt-to-income ratios, and down payments.

2. **Larger Down Payments:** Conventional loans often require larger down payments, with 20% down payment being standard to avoid private mortgage insurance (PMI).

3. **Limited Assistance Programs:** Conventional loans may not offer as many down payment assistance programs as government-backed loans.

Best Suited For: Conventional loans are best suited for borrowers with good to excellent credit scores (typically 620 or higher) and stable financial backgrounds who can afford a larger down payment. They are also ideal for borrowers purchasing higher-priced homes that exceed the loan limits for government-backed loans.

Realtor Guidance: When communicating with homebuyers, realtors should emphasize the flexibility and potentially lower costs associated with conventional loans, especially for borrowers with strong credit histories. They should also highlight the importance of being financially prepared to meet the higher down payment requirements and suggest exploring different loan options to find the best fit for their individual circumstances.

Non-Conventional Loans

Description: Non-conventional loans, also known as non-QM (Qualified Mortgage) loans, do not meet the criteria set by Fannie Mae and Freddie Mac. They may include various types of loans, such as jumbo loans, interest-only loans, and alternative documentation loans.

Pros:
1. **Flexible Qualification Criteria:** Non-conventional loans may offer more lenient qualification requirements, including lower credit score thresholds and higher debt-to-income ratios.

2. **Unique Financing Options:** Non-conventional loans may provide alternative financing options, such as interest-only payments or financing for non-standard properties.

3. **Opportunity for Unique Situations:** Non-conventional loans can be beneficial for borrowers with unique financial situations or property types that do not meet conventional loan standards.

Cons:
1. **Higher Interest Rates:** Non-conventional loans may come with higher interest rates and fees compared to conventional loans, reflecting the increased risk to lenders.

2. **Limited Availability:** Non-conventional loans may be less widely available and offered by fewer lenders compared to conventional loans.

3. **Potential for Payment Shocks:** Some non-conventional loans, such as interest-only loans, may have payment structures that result in higher payments or payment shocks in the future.

Best Suited For: Non-conventional loans are best suited for borrowers who may not qualify for conventional financing due to unique circumstances, such as self-employed individuals with fluctuating incomes, borrowers with credit challenges, or those purchasing non-standard properties.

Realtor Guidance: Realtors should educate homebuyers about the potential benefits and drawbacks of non-conventional loans, emphasizing the importance of understanding the specific terms and requirements of these loans. They should encourage borrowers to explore non-conventional options if they have unique financial situations or property needs that may not align with conventional loan standards. Additionally, realtors should recommend working with experienced loan officers who specialize in non-conventional lending to navigate the process effectively.

Jumbo Loans

Description: Jumbo loans are mortgage loans that exceed the conforming loan limits set by Fannie Mae and Freddie Mac. These loans are used to finance higher-priced properties that exceed the maximum loan limits established for conventional loans. Jumbo loans are typically offered by private lenders and may have stricter qualification criteria compared to conventional loans.

Pros:
1. **Financing High-Value Properties:** Jumbo loans allow borrowers to finance properties that exceed the loan limits for conventional loans, enabling them to purchase luxury homes or properties in high-cost areas.

2. **Flexibility:** Jumbo loans offer flexibility in terms of loan amounts, allowing borrowers to finance larger purchases without the need for multiple mortgages.

3. **Competitive Interest Rates:** Despite being larger loans, jumbo loan interest rates can be competitive, especially for borrowers with strong credit scores and financial backgrounds.

Cons:
1. **Stricter Qualification Requirements:** Jumbo loans often have stricter qualification criteria, including higher credit score requirements, lower debt-to-income ratios, and larger down payments.

2. **Higher Costs:** Jumbo loans may come with higher interest rates, fees, and closing costs compared to conventional loans, reflecting the increased risk to lenders.

3. **Limited Availability:** Jumbo loans may be less widely available and offered by fewer lenders compared to conventional loans, making it important for borrowers to shop around for the best terms.

Best Suited For: Jumbo loans are best suited for borrowers who are purchasing high-value properties that exceed the loan limits for conventional loans. They are typically used by affluent buyers, investors, or individuals purchasing luxury homes in upscale neighborhoods or high-cost areas.

Realtor Guidance: When communicating with homebuyers, realtors should educate them about the availability and requirements of jumbo loans, especially if they are considering purchasing high-value properties. Realtors should emphasize the importance of working with experienced loan officers who specialize in jumbo lending to navigate the process effectively and secure competitive terms. Additionally, realtors should advise borrowers to prepare for stricter qualification requirements and potentially higher costs associated with jumbo loans compared to conventional financing options.

Fixed-Rate Loans

Description: Fixed-rate loans are a type of mortgage loan where the interest rate remains constant throughout the entire term of the loan. This means that the borrower's monthly principal and interest payments remain unchanged for the duration of the loan, providing predictability and stability in housing expenses.

Pros:

1. **Rate Stability:** The main advantage of fixed-rate loans is that borrowers are protected from fluctuations in interest rates. Regardless of changes in the broader economy or financial markets, the borrower's interest rate remains fixed, providing peace of mind and predictability in budgeting.

2. **Budgeting Certainty:** With fixed monthly payments, borrowers can accurately budget their housing expenses over the life of the loan, making it easier to manage household finances and plan for future expenses.

3. **Long-Term Savings:** Fixed-rate loans allow borrowers to lock in a low interest rate for the entire loan term, potentially saving them money over time compared to adjustable-rate or variable-rate loans if interest rates rise in the future.

Cons:

1. **Higher Initial Rates:** Fixed-rate loans typically have slightly higher initial interest rates compared to adjustable-rate loans, as borrowers pay a premium for the stability and predictability of fixed monthly payments.

2. **Limited Short-Term Savings:** While fixed-rate loans offer long-term rate stability, borrowers may miss out on potential short-term savings if interest rates decline after they lock in their rate.

3. **Potential Refinancing Costs:** If interest rates decrease significantly after obtaining a fixed-rate loan, borrowers may consider refinancing to secure a lower rate. However, refinancing involves closing costs and fees, which can offset some of the potential savings.

Best Suited For: Fixed-rate loans are best suited for borrowers who prioritize stability and prefer the security of knowing their monthly payments will remain constant over the life of the loan. They are particularly well-suited for homebuyers planning to stay in their homes for an extended period or those who are risk-averse and want to avoid the uncertainty associated with adjustable-rate loans.

Realtor Guidance: When communicating with homebuyers, realtors should highlight the benefits of fixed-rate loans, such as rate stability and long-term savings potential. Realtors can reassure buyers that fixed-rate loans offer protection against rising interest rates, providing stability in housing expenses and making it easier to plan for the future. Additionally, realtors should encourage borrowers to work closely with experienced loan officers to explore fixed-rate loan options and secure competitive interest rates that meet their financial goals and preferences.

Adjustable-Rate Loans

Description: Adjustable-rate loans, also known as variable-rate loans or ARMs, are mortgage loans where the interest rate fluctuates over time based on changes in a specified financial index, such as the prime rate or LIBOR (London Interbank Offered Rate). Typically, adjustable-rate loans have an initial fixed-rate period, followed by periodic adjustments based on predetermined intervals, such as annually or semi-annually.

Pros:

1. **Lower Initial Rates:** Adjustable-rate loans often feature lower initial interest rates compared to fixed-rate loans, making them attractive to borrowers seeking lower initial monthly payments or short-term savings.

2. **Potential for Rate Decreases:** If interest rates decline in the future, borrowers with adjustable-rate loans may benefit from lower monthly payments during the adjustment periods, resulting in potential cost savings over time.

3. **Flexibility:** Adjustable-rate loans offer flexibility for borrowers who plan to sell or refinance their homes before the end of the initial fixed-rate period. Borrowers can take advantage of lower initial rates and then sell or refinance before the first adjustment occurs.

Cons:
1. **Rate Volatility:** One of the main drawbacks of adjustable-rate loans is the potential for interest rate volatility. As interest rates fluctuate, borrowers may experience significant increases in their monthly payments during adjustment periods, leading to financial uncertainty and higher housing expenses.

2. **Payment Shock:** Borrowers may experience payment shock if interest rates rise substantially during adjustment periods, resulting in higher monthly mortgage payments that may strain their budget and financial resources.

3. **Risk of Negative Amortization:** Some adjustable-rate loans come with the risk of negative amortization, where the borrower's monthly payments may not cover the full amount of interest owed, leading to an increase in the loan balance over time.

Best Suited For: Adjustable-rate loans are best suited for borrowers who prioritize short-term savings, plan to sell or refinance their homes within the initial fixed-rate period, or expect interest rates to decline in the future. They may also be suitable for borrowers who can tolerate some level of risk and volatility in exchange for lower initial monthly payments.

Realtor Guidance: When discussing adjustable-rate loans with homebuyers, realtors should emphasize the lower initial rates and potential short-term savings offered by these loans. However, realtors should also educate buyers about the risks associated with adjustable-rate loans, such as payment volatility and potential rate increases in the future. Realtors can encourage borrowers to carefully consider their financial goals and risk tolerance before choosing an adjustable-rate loan, and to work closely with experienced loan officers to explore all available loan options and make informed decisions.

FHA Loans

Description: FHA (Federal Housing Administration) loans are mortgage loans insured by the federal government, specifically designed to assist borrowers with lower credit scores and limited down payment capabilities. These loans are issued by FHA-approved lenders and are popular among first-time homebuyers and those with less-than-perfect credit.

Pros:
1. **Low Down Payment:** One of the primary advantages of FHA loans is the low down payment requirement, which can be as low as 3.5% of the purchase price. This makes homeownership more accessible to borrowers who may struggle to save for a large down payment.

2. **Flexible Credit Requirements:** FHA loans are more lenient when it comes to credit requirements compared to conventional loans. Borrowers with less-than-perfect credit scores may still qualify for an FHA loan, making it an attractive option for those with limited credit history or past financial challenges.

3. **Competitive Interest Rates:** FHA loans typically offer competitive interest rates, allowing borrowers to secure affordable financing for their home purchase.

4. **Assumable:** FHA loans are assumable, meaning that if the borrower decides to sell their home, the buyer can take over the existing FHA loan, potentially making the property more appealing to potential buyers.

Cons:
1. **Mortgage Insurance Premiums (MIP):** FHA loans require both an upfront mortgage insurance premium (UFMIP) and an annual mortgage insurance premium (MIP), which increase the overall

cost of the loan. Borrowers must pay the MIP for the life of the loan if the down payment is less than 10%, or for the first 11 years if the down payment is 10% or more.

2. **Loan Limits:** FHA loans have maximum loan limits set by the FHA, which may vary depending on the location of the property. Borrowers purchasing homes above the FHA loan limits may need to consider alternative financing options.

3. **Property Standards:** FHA loans require the property to meet certain minimum property standards set by the FHA. Homes that do not meet these standards may require repairs or renovations before qualifying for FHA financing.

Best Suited For: FHA loans are best suited for first-time homebuyers, borrowers with limited down payment funds, or those with less-than-perfect credit. They may also be suitable for borrowers purchasing homes in areas with higher home prices, as FHA loan limits are generally higher in these areas.

Realtor Guidance: When discussing FHA loans with homebuyers, realtors should highlight the low down payment requirement and flexible credit criteria offered by FHA loans. Realtors can also inform buyers about the potential for higher mortgage insurance premiums and loan limits associated with FHA financing. Additionally, realtors can recommend working with experienced loan officers familiar with FHA loan requirements to navigate the application process smoothly and ensure a successful home purchase.

VA Loans

Description: VA (Veterans Affairs) loans are mortgage loans guaranteed by the U.S. Department of Veterans Affairs, available to eligible active-duty service members, veterans, and surviving spouses. These loans are designed to provide affordable financing options to those who have served or are currently serving in the military.

Pros:
1. **No Down Payment:** One of the most significant benefits of VA loans is that eligible borrowers can purchase a home with no down payment, making homeownership more accessible, especially for first-time homebuyers.

2. **No Private Mortgage Insurance (PMI):** Unlike conventional loans, VA loans do not require borrowers to pay private mortgage insurance (PMI), which can result in significant cost savings over the life of the loan.

3. **Competitive Interest Rates:** VA loans typically offer competitive interest rates, often lower than those available with conventional loans, helping borrowers save money on their monthly mortgage payments.

4. **Flexible Credit Requirements:** VA loans have more lenient credit requirements compared to conventional loans, making them accessible to borrowers with less-than-perfect credit or limited credit history.

5. **No Prepayment Penalty:** VA loans do not impose prepayment penalties, allowing borrowers to pay off their mortgage early without incurring additional fees.

Cons:
1. **Funding Fee:** VA loans may require a one-time funding fee, which is a percentage of the loan amount. While this fee helps offset the cost of the VA loan program, it adds to the upfront costs of obtaining a VA loan.

2. **Property Eligibility Requirements:** VA loans have specific property eligibility requirements, including minimum property standards and appraisal guidelines. Homes must meet these requirements to qualify for VA financing.

3. **Limited Eligibility:** VA loans are only available to eligible active-duty service members, veterans, and surviving spouses, limiting access to those who have served or are currently serving in the military.

Best Suited For: VA loans are best suited for eligible active-duty service members, veterans, and surviving spouses who meet the VA's eligibility criteria. These loans are particularly beneficial for those who may not have significant savings for a down payment or who want to avoid paying private mortgage insurance.

Realtor Guidance: Realtors can highlight the advantages of VA loans, such as the ability to purchase a home with no down payment and competitive interest rates, when working with military clients or veterans. Realtors should also inform buyers about the funding fee associated with VA loans and ensure that the chosen property meets VA eligibility requirements. Additionally, realtors can recommend connecting with VA-approved lenders experienced in handling VA loan transactions to streamline the homebuying process and maximize the benefits of VA financing.

USDA Loans

Description: USDA (United States Department of Agriculture) loans, also known as Rural Development loans, are mortgage loans offered to eligible homebuyers in rural and suburban areas by the USDA's Rural Development program. These loans aim to promote homeownership in designated rural and suburban communities by providing affordable financing options to low- and moderate-income households.

Pros:
1. **No Down Payment:** One of the primary advantages of USDA loans is that eligible borrowers can purchase a home with no down payment, making homeownership more accessible, especially for first-time buyers with limited savings.

2. **Low Interest Rates:** USDA loans often offer competitive interest rates compared to conventional loans, helping borrowers save money on their monthly mortgage payments over the life of the loan.

3. **Flexible Credit Requirements:** USDA loans have more lenient credit requirements compared to conventional loans, making them accessible to borrowers with less-than-perfect credit or limited credit history.

4. **No Private Mortgage Insurance (PMI):** USDA loans do not require borrowers to pay private mortgage insurance (PMI), which can result in significant cost savings over time.

5. **Closing Cost Assistance:** USDA loans may allow borrowers to finance their closing costs into the loan amount or negotiate seller concessions, reducing the out-of-pocket expenses associated with closing on a home.

Cons:

1. **Geographic Restrictions:** USDA loans are only available for properties located in eligible rural and suburban areas designated by the USDA. Borrowers must ensure that the property they intend to purchase meets the USDA's location requirements to qualify for financing.

2. **Income Limits:** USDA loans have income limits based on the area's median income, and borrowers must meet these income restrictions to be eligible for the program. Higher-income individuals may not qualify for USDA financing.

3. **Funding Fee:** USDA loans may require a one-time upfront funding fee and an annual fee, which are used to fund the USDA's Rural Development program. While these fees help support the program, they add to the upfront costs of obtaining a USDA loan.

Best Suited For: USDA loans are best suited for low- and moderate-income homebuyers looking to purchase homes in eligible rural and suburban areas. These loans are particularly beneficial for individuals and families who may not have significant savings for a down payment or who prefer to avoid paying private mortgage insurance.

Realtor Guidance: Realtors can highlight the advantages of USDA loans, such as the opportunity to purchase a home with no down payment and competitive interest rates, when working with buyers interested in homes located in rural or suburban areas. Realtors should educate buyers about the USDA's geographic and income eligibility requirements and help them determine whether a property qualifies for USDA financing. Additionally, realtors can recommend connecting with USDA-approved lenders experienced in handling USDA loan transactions to navigate the application process smoothly and efficiently.

Alternative documentation loans

Description: Alternative documentation loans offer flexibility in the mortgage application process by allowing borrowers to provide alternative forms of income verification instead of traditional documentation like tax returns and pay stubs. Here's a detailed exploration of various alternative documentation loans, their pros and cons, and their suitability for different types of borrowers, along with insights on how realtors can effectively communicate this information to home buyers:

1. **Bank Statement Loans:** Bank statement loans allow borrowers to qualify for a mortgage based on their bank statements rather than traditional income documentation. Lenders typically review 12 to 24 months of bank statements to assess the borrower's income and determine their eligibility.

   - **Pros:**
     1. Suitable for self-employed individuals or those with irregular income streams.
     2. Offers flexibility for borrowers who may not have consistent pay stubs or tax returns.
     3. Allows borrowers to qualify based on actual cash flow rather than reported income.
   - **Cons:**
     1. May come with higher interest rates or fees compared to conventional loans.
     2. Borrowers may need to provide additional documentation to explain large deposits or unusual transactions.
     3. Lenders may require higher down payments or reserves to mitigate risk.

   - **Best Suited For:** Self-employed individuals, freelancers, small business owners, and borrowers with non-traditional income sources.

2. **1099 Only Loans:** 1099 only loans cater to borrowers who receive income as independent contractors or freelancers and file IRS Form 1099 instead of W-2s. These loans allow borrowers to qualify based on their 1099 income.

   - **Pros:**
     1. Provides options for borrowers with non-traditional employment arrangements.
     2. Allows borrowers to leverage their 1099 income without traditional W-2 documentation.
     3. May offer flexibility in income verification requirements.
   - **Cons:**
     1. Borrowers may face higher interest rates or stricter eligibility criteria.

2. Lenders may require a larger down payment or stronger credit history.
3. Limited availability compared to conventional loans.

- **Best Suited For:** Independent contractors, freelancers, gig workers, and individuals with diverse income sources.

3. **W2 Only Loans:** W2 only loans are designed for borrowers who receive income as employees and have W-2 forms as their primary income documentation. These loans streamline the application process by focusing solely on W-2 income.

   - **Pros:**
     1. Simplifies income verification for salaried employees with stable income.
     2. Allows borrowers to qualify based on their W-2 earnings without additional documentation.
     3. May offer competitive interest rates and terms similar to conventional loans.
   - **Cons:**
     1. Limited flexibility for borrowers with additional income sources or irregular earnings.
     2. May not be suitable for self-employed individuals or those with non-W-2 income.
     3. Borrowers still need to meet credit and debt-to-income requirements.

   - **Best Suited For:** Salaried employees with stable jobs and consistent W-2 income.

4. **1 Year Tax Return Only Loans:** These loans consider a borrower's income based solely on their most recent year's tax return, providing an alternative to traditional two-year tax return requirements. Borrowers must have sufficient income reported on their tax return to qualify.

   - **Pros:**
     1. Simplifies income verification by focusing on the most recent tax return.
     2. Suitable for borrowers with a significant increase in income or recent career change.

3. Offers flexibility for those who may not have two years of tax returns due to life events.
- **Cons:**
  1. Borrowers may face higher interest rates or stricter eligibility criteria.
  2. Lenders may require additional documentation to verify income stability.
  3. Limited availability and may vary among lenders.

- **Best Suited For:** Borrowers with increasing income trends, recent career changes, or those who experienced a temporary decline in income.

5. **P&L Only Loans:** Profit and loss (P&L) only loans are tailored for self-employed borrowers who report income through business profit and loss statements instead of traditional tax returns. Lenders evaluate the borrower's business revenue and expenses to determine income eligibility.

- **Pros:**
  1. Allows self-employed individuals to qualify based on business income without tax returns.
  2. Provides flexibility for borrowers with fluctuating business income or deductions.
  3. May offer competitive terms and options for business owners.
- **Cons:**
  1. Requires thorough documentation of business financials, including profit and loss statements.
  2. Borrowers may encounter stricter underwriting criteria or higher interest rates.
  3. Lenders may require a larger down payment or reserves to mitigate risk.

- **Best Suited For:** Self-employed individuals, entrepreneurs, and small business owners who report income through P&L statements.

Realtor Guidance: In communicating this information to home buyers, realtors play a crucial role in helping them understand the diverse options available for mortgage financing. By discussing the pros and cons of each alternative documentation loan type, realtors can assist home buyers in identifying the most suitable option based on their employment status, income sources, and financial goals. Realtors should emphasize the importance of consulting with mortgage professionals to explore the available loan programs and determine the best fit for their specific circumstances. Additionally, realtors can provide

Investor Loans

In the realm of mortgage lending, investor loans and Debt-Service Coverage Ratio (DSCR) loans stand out as specialized financing options tailored for distinct purposes and borrower profiles. Let's delve into each, exploring their intricacies, advantages, limitations, and ideal candidates, with a focus on how realtors can leverage this knowledge to guide their clients effectively.

Investor Loans:
Description: Investor loans, as the name implies, are designed for real estate investors seeking to purchase properties for rental income or capital appreciation. These loans typically feature unique terms and conditions tailored to accommodate the needs and risk profiles of investors, such as higher down payments and interest rates compared to traditional mortgages.

Pros:
1. **Potential for High Returns:** Real estate investment offers the potential for lucrative returns through rental income and property appreciation.

2. **Diversification:** Investors can diversify their investment portfolios by allocating funds to real estate, reducing overall risk.

3. **Tax Benefits:** Investors may benefit from tax deductions on mortgage interest, property taxes, and depreciation, enhancing overall returns.

Cons:
1. **Higher Costs:** Investor loans often come with higher interest rates, down payment requirements, and closing costs, increasing the overall cost of financing.

2. **Risks:** Real estate investing carries inherent risks, including vacancy periods, property depreciation, and market fluctuations.

3. **Qualification Criteria:** Lenders may impose stricter qualification criteria for investor loans, including higher credit score requirements and lower debt-to-income ratios.

Best Suited For: Investor loans are ideal for individuals or entities seeking to build wealth through real estate investment. They are suited for experienced investors with sufficient capital reserves and a long-term investment horizon.

Realtor Guidance: Realtors can play a pivotal role in guiding investor clients by providing insights into local market trends, rental demand, and potential rental income. They can also facilitate connections with lenders specializing in investor loans and offer recommendations for property management services to optimize investment returns.

Debt-Service Coverage Ratio (DSCR) Loans

Description: Debt-Service Coverage Ratio (DSCR) loans are a specialized form of financing primarily used for commercial real estate investments. Unlike traditional mortgages that focus on the borrower's creditworthiness, DSCR loans primarily evaluate the property's income-generating potential to determine loan eligibility.

Pros:
1. **Property-Centric Evaluation:** DSCR loans assess the property's ability to generate sufficient income to cover loan payments, reducing reliance on the borrower's personal finances.

2. **Higher Loan Amounts:** DSCR loans may allow borrowers to qualify for higher loan amounts based on the property's income potential, enabling them to pursue larger investment opportunities.

3. **Flexible Terms:** DSCR loans offer flexibility in terms of loan structure, repayment schedules, and interest rates, allowing borrowers to tailor financing to their specific needs.

Cons:

1. **Stringent Requirements:** DSCR loans may require extensive documentation and rigorous property evaluation, leading to longer approval processes and higher upfront costs.

2. **Limited Availability:** DSCR loans are less common in the residential mortgage market and may be offered by specialized lenders catering to commercial real estate investors.

3. **Risk Exposure:** Borrowers assume the risk of rental income fluctuations, property vacancies, and market downturns, which can affect the property's ability to generate sufficient cash flow.

Best Suited For: DSCR loans are best suited for experienced real estate investors seeking to finance income-producing properties such as multifamily buildings, commercial complexes, or rental properties. They are ideal for investors with a thorough understanding of property management and rental market dynamics.

Realtor Guidance: Realtors can assist clients in identifying suitable investment properties with strong income potential and understanding the nuances of DSCR financing. They can also facilitate connections with lenders specializing in commercial real estate loans and provide insights into market conditions and investment strategies tailored to the client's objectives. By leveraging their expertise and network, realtors can empower investors to make informed decisions and achieve their investment goals.

Investor loans and DSCR loans offer distinct opportunities for real estate investors to expand their portfolios and maximize returns. By understanding the nuances of these financing options and collaborating closely with their realtors, investors can navigate the complexities of real estate investing with confidence and achieve long-term success.

CDFI Loans: Empowering Communities Through Affordable Housing

Description: Community Development Financial Institutions (CDFIs) play a crucial role in providing access to affordable housing financing for underserved communities and low-to-moderate-income households. CDFI home loans are financial products offered by these specialized institutions, aiming to promote homeownership and community development in economically disadvantaged areas. These loans often feature flexible terms, lower down payment requirements, and supportive services to help borrowers overcome barriers to homeownership.

Pros:

1. **Increased Access to Financing:** CDFI home loans expand access to homeownership for individuals and families who may face challenges qualifying for traditional mortgages.

2. **Flexible Terms:** CDFIs offer flexible loan terms, including lower down payment requirements, reduced closing costs, and alternative credit evaluation methods, making homeownership more attainable.

3. **Community Development:** By providing affordable housing financing, CDFIs contribute to neighborhood stabilization, economic revitalization, and wealth building within underserved communities.

4. **Supportive Services:** CDFIs often offer supportive services such as financial counseling, homebuyer education, and post-purchase assistance to help borrowers navigate the homeownership process successfully.

Cons:

1. **Limited Availability:** CDFI home loans may be limited in availability and geographic scope, primarily targeting specific underserved communities and regions.

2. **Stringent Eligibility Criteria:** While CDFIs aim to serve low-to-moderate-income borrowers, they may still have eligibility criteria related to income, credit history, and property location.

3. **Potential for Longer Approval Process:** Due to the focus on serving underserved communities and the use of alternative underwriting methods, the approval process for CDFI home loans may take longer compared to traditional mortgages.

Best Suited For: CDFI home loans are best suited for individuals and families seeking affordable homeownership options in underserved communities or those facing financial barriers to traditional mortgage financing. They are particularly beneficial for low-to-moderate-income households, first-time homebuyers, and individuals with limited credit history.

Realtor Guidance: Realtors play a crucial role in connecting homebuyers with CDFI home loan programs and educating them about the benefits and eligibility requirements. They can help identify CDFIs operating in the local area, assist clients in accessing resources for financial counseling and homebuyer education, and advocate for affordable housing initiatives within the community. By partnering with CDFIs and promoting access to affordable homeownership opportunities, realtors can contribute to equitable housing access and community development efforts.

CDFI home loans serve as a vital tool in expanding homeownership opportunities and promoting economic empowerment in underserved communities. With their focus on affordability, flexibility, and community development, these loans offer a pathway to sustainable homeownership for individuals and families striving to achieve their housing goals. By leveraging their expertise and networks, realtors can help bridge the gap between homebuyers and CDFI home loan programs, fostering inclusive and thriving communities.

No Income Community Mortgages

Description: No Income Community Mortgages are specialized mortgage products designed to provide access to homeownership for individuals and families who may not have traditional sources of income documentation, such as W-2 forms or tax returns. These mortgages are tailored for underserved communities and prioritize factors other than income verification in the loan approval process. Instead, lenders focus on factors such as credit history, assets, and the property's value to assess the borrower's ability to repay the loan.

Pros:
1. **Expanded Access:** No Income Community Mortgages expand access to homeownership for individuals and families who may have difficulty documenting their income through traditional means.
2. **Flexibility:** These mortgages offer flexibility in income verification requirements, allowing borrowers to qualify based on alternative factors such as assets, rental history, or employment status.
3. **Community Development:** By facilitating homeownership in underserved communities, No Income Community Mortgages

contribute to neighborhood stabilization, wealth building, and economic revitalization.
4. **Diverse Applicant Pool:** These mortgages attract a diverse applicant pool, including self-employed individuals, freelancers, gig economy workers, and individuals with irregular income streams.

Cons:
1. **Higher Interest Rates:** No Income Community Mortgages may come with higher interest rates or additional fees compared to traditional mortgages, reflecting the higher risk associated with limited income documentation.
2. **Stricter Eligibility Requirements:** While income verification criteria may be relaxed, borrowers still need to meet other eligibility requirements, such as credit score thresholds, down payment obligations, and debt-to-income ratios.
3. **Limited Availability:** No Income Community Mortgages may be offered by a limited number of lenders and may have specific geographic or property eligibility requirements.

Best Suited For: No Income Community Mortgages are best suited for individuals and families in underserved communities who have difficulty documenting their income through traditional means. They are particularly beneficial for self-employed individuals, freelancers, seasonal workers, and individuals with non-traditional employment arrangements. These mortgages also cater to first-time homebuyers and individuals with limited credit history or past financial challenges.

Realtor Guidance: Realtors play a crucial role in educating homebuyers about the availability and benefits of No Income Community Mortgages. They can assist clients in identifying lenders offering these specialized mortgage products and guide them through the application process. Realtors should emphasize the importance of understanding the terms, interest rates, and eligibility requirements associated with No Income Community Mortgages to ensure informed decision-making. By advocating for access to alternative mortgage options and supporting clients in navigating the complexities of homeownership financing, realtors contribute to expanding housing opportunities and fostering inclusive communities.

No Income Community Mortgages serve as a valuable tool in promoting equitable access to homeownership and addressing the needs of underserved populations. Despite their potential drawbacks, these specialized mortgage products offer a pathway to homeownership for individuals and families with diverse income profiles. Realtors play a pivotal role in connecting homebuyers with No Income Community Mortgage opportunities and empowering them to achieve their homeownership goals. Through collaboration with lenders and community organizations, realtors can help break down barriers to homeownership and create pathways to sustainable housing solutions for all.

Interest-Only Loans

Description: Interest-only loans are a type of mortgage loan where the borrower is only required to pay the interest on the loan for a specified period, typically ranging from 5 to 10 years. During this initial period, the borrower's monthly payments consist solely of interest, and they do not make any principal payments. After the interest-only period ends, the loan typically converts to a fully amortizing loan, and the borrower begins making payments that include both principal and interest.

Pros:
1. Lower Initial Payments: With interest-only loans, borrowers benefit from lower initial monthly payments during the interest-only period, making homeownership more affordable, especially in the early years of the loan.
2. Cash Flow Flexibility: Interest-only loans provide borrowers with flexibility in managing their cash flow, allowing them to allocate funds to other expenses or investments during the interest-only period.
3. Potential Tax Benefits: In some cases, borrowers may be able to deduct the interest portion of their mortgage payments from their taxable income, potentially providing tax advantages.

Cons:
1. Higher Long-Term Costs: While interest-only loans offer lower initial payments, borrowers end up paying more in interest over the life of the loan compared to fully amortizing loans, as they do not make any principal payments during the interest-only period.
2. Payment Shock: When the interest-only period ends and the loan converts to a fully amortizing loan, borrowers may experience a significant increase in their monthly payments, leading to payment shock and potential financial strain.

3. Limited Availability: Interest-only loans may be less common and offered by fewer lenders compared to traditional mortgage options, limiting the choices available to borrowers.

Best Suited For: Interest-only loans are best suited for borrowers who expect their income to increase in the future or who have irregular income streams, such as self-employed individuals or those with fluctuating earnings. They may also be suitable for borrowers who plan to sell or refinance their property before the end of the interest-only period.

Realtor Guidance: When communicating with homebuyers, realtors should educate them about the features and potential risks of interest-only loans. Realtors should advise borrowers to carefully consider their financial situation and long-term goals before opting for an interest-only loan, emphasizing the importance of understanding how the loan works and the implications of the transition to full principal and interest payments after the interest-only period ends. Additionally, realtors should encourage borrowers to work closely with knowledgeable loan officers to explore all available mortgage options and select the most appropriate financing solution for their needs.

Reverse Mortgages

Description: Reverse mortgages are special types of home loans available to homeowners aged 62 and older that allow them to convert a portion of their home equity into cash. Unlike traditional mortgages where borrowers make monthly payments to the lender, reverse mortgages provide homeowners with the option to receive loan proceeds as a lump sum, fixed monthly payments, a line of credit, or a combination of these methods. The loan is repaid when the borrower sells the home, moves out permanently, or passes away, with the loan balance typically paid off using the proceeds from the sale of the home.

Pros:
1. Supplemental Income: Reverse mortgages provide homeowners with a valuable source of supplemental income, allowing them to tap into their home equity to cover living expenses, medical bills, or other financial needs during retirement.
2. No Monthly Mortgage Payments: Unlike traditional mortgages, reverse mortgage borrowers are not required to make monthly

mortgage payments to the lender. Instead, they can receive loan proceeds without adding to their monthly financial obligations.

3. Loan Flexibility: Reverse mortgages offer flexibility in how homeowners can receive their loan proceeds, including options for lump-sum payments, monthly installments, lines of credit, or a combination of these payment methods.

4. Homeownership Retention: Reverse mortgages allow homeowners to remain in their homes while accessing their equity, providing them with the opportunity to age in place and maintain their quality of life.

5. Non-Recourse Loan: Reverse mortgages are non-recourse loans, which means that borrowers (or their heirs) are not personally liable for any loan balance that exceeds the value of the home when it is sold to repay the loan.

Cons:

1. Accrued Interest: Since reverse mortgage borrowers do not make monthly payments, the interest on the loan accumulates over time and is added to the loan balance, potentially reducing the equity available to heirs when the home is sold.

2. Fees and Closing Costs: Reverse mortgages often come with upfront fees and closing costs, including origination fees, mortgage insurance premiums, appraisal fees, and closing costs, which can increase the overall cost of the loan.

3. Impact on Heirs: Reverse mortgages can affect the inheritance of heirs, as the loan balance must be repaid from the proceeds of the home sale after the borrower's death. Depending on the loan balance and home value, heirs may need to sell the home to satisfy the debt.

4. Home Equity Depletion: Using a reverse mortgage to access home equity can deplete the equity available to homeowners, potentially limiting their ability to leave an inheritance or access additional funds for future needs.

Best Suited For: Reverse mortgages are best suited for older homeowners who have significant home equity and want to supplement their retirement income without selling their home. These loans are particularly beneficial for individuals who plan to remain in their homes long-term and have limited sources of retirement income.

Realtor Guidance: Realtors should educate older homebuyers about the pros and cons of reverse mortgages and encourage them to consider their long-term financial goals and needs before pursuing this financing option. Realtors can help clients explore alternatives to reverse mortgages, such as downsizing to a more affordable home or accessing other sources of retirement income, to meet their financial objectives while preserving home equity for themselves or their heirs. Additionally, realtors can refer clients to reputable reverse mortgage lenders and financial advisors who specialize in retirement planning to ensure they make informed decisions about their housing and financial futures.

Energy-Efficient Mortgages (EEMs)

Description: Energy-Efficient Mortgages (EEMs) are specialized mortgage products that enable homebuyers to finance energy-efficient improvements or upgrades to a property as part of their home purchase or refinance loan. These mortgages incentivize energy-efficient home upgrades by allowing borrowers to finance the cost of improvements into their mortgage loan, providing upfront funds to make energy-saving enhancements without the need for additional financing.

Pros:
1. Lower Utility Costs: Energy-efficient improvements financed through EEMs can result in reduced energy consumption and lower utility bills for homeowners over time, leading to potential long-term cost savings and increased affordability.
2. Enhanced Comfort and Health: Energy-efficient upgrades, such as improved insulation, energy-efficient windows, and high-efficiency heating and cooling systems, can enhance indoor comfort levels and promote healthier living environments for occupants.
3. Increased Property Value: Energy-efficient features and upgrades can enhance the market value and resale potential of a property, appealing to eco-conscious homebuyers and contributing to a higher appraised value.
4. Environmental Benefits: EEMs support environmentally sustainable homeownership by encouraging energy-efficient building practices and reducing greenhouse gas emissions associated with energy consumption, contributing to a greener and more sustainable future.
5. Financing Flexibility: EEMs offer borrowers flexibility in financing energy-efficient improvements, allowing them to include the cost of upgrades in their mortgage loan without

requiring additional cash reserves or loans, simplifying the home improvement process.

Cons:
1. Upfront Costs: While energy-efficient improvements can lead to long-term savings, the upfront costs of purchasing and installing energy-efficient upgrades may be higher compared to conventional options, requiring borrowers to consider the initial investment and weigh the long-term benefits.
2. Limited Eligibility: Not all properties or energy-efficient upgrades may qualify for EEM financing, and eligibility requirements may vary depending on the lender, loan program, and energy efficiency standards, potentially limiting access for some borrowers.
3. Appraisal Challenges: Appraising the value of energy-efficient features and upgrades can be challenging, as their impact on property value may vary based on local market conditions, appraiser expertise, and buyer preferences, potentially affecting loan approval and financing terms.
4. Additional Documentation: Participating in an EEM program may require borrowers to provide additional documentation, such as energy audits, contractor estimates, or verification of energy-efficient features, which can add complexity to the loan application and approval process.
5. Potential Resale Limitations: While energy-efficient upgrades can enhance property value, their impact on resale value and marketability may vary, depending on buyer preferences, market trends, and the perceived value of energy-efficient features, potentially limiting resale opportunities in certain markets.

Best Suited For: Energy-Efficient Mortgages (EEMs) are best suited for homebuyers and homeowners who prioritize energy efficiency, sustainability, and long-term cost savings. These mortgages are ideal for individuals and families seeking to finance energy-efficient upgrades as part of their home purchase or refinance loan, including first-time homebuyers, eco-conscious buyers, and homeowners looking to improve energy efficiency and comfort in their existing homes.

Realtor Guidance: Realtors play a vital role in educating homebuyers about the benefits of Energy-Efficient Mortgages (EEMs) and highlighting energy-efficient features and upgrades that can enhance property value and appeal. Realtors can guide clients in exploring EEM financing options, explaining eligibility requirements, and connecting them with lenders and energy efficiency experts to assess the feasibility and cost-effectiveness of energy-efficient upgrades. Additionally, realtors can showcase energy-efficient homes, highlight their benefits during property tours, and emphasize the long-term cost savings and environmental advantages of energy-efficient homeownership. By promoting EEMs and energy-efficient features, realtors can help clients make informed decisions about financing and prioritize sustainability and energy efficiency in their homebuying journey.

Down Payment Assistance (DPA) Programs

Description: Down Payment Assistance (DPA) programs are initiatives offered by government agencies, non-profit organizations, and housing finance authorities to help homebuyers overcome the financial barrier of making a down payment when purchasing a home. These programs provide eligible borrowers with grants, loans, or forgivable loans to cover part or all of their down payment and closing costs, making homeownership more accessible to individuals and families with limited financial resources.

Pros:
1. Increased Affordability: DPA programs reduce the upfront costs associated with purchasing a home, making homeownership more affordable and accessible to low- and moderate-income homebuyers.
2. Expanded Homeownership Opportunities: DPA programs open doors to homeownership for individuals and families who may not have been able to save enough for a down payment on their own, including first-time homebuyers, minority populations, and households with limited savings.
3. Financial Flexibility: DPA funds can be used in conjunction with other mortgage financing options, such as FHA, VA, and conventional loans, allowing borrowers to secure favorable terms and interest rates without the need for a large down payment.
4. Potential for Forgiveness: Some DPA programs offer grants or forgivable loans that do not need to be repaid if the borrower meets certain eligibility criteria, such as residing in the home for a specified period.
5. Stimulated Housing Market: By assisting qualified homebuyers with down payment funds, DPA programs contribute to the stability and growth of the housing market, encouraging

homeownership and supporting economic development in communities.

Cons:

1. Eligibility Requirements: DPA programs often have specific eligibility criteria related to income limits, credit scores, home purchase price limits, and participation in homeownership education courses, which may limit access for certain borrowers.
2. Limited Funding Availability: DPA programs may have limited funding allocations or operate on a first-come, first-served basis, leading to potential delays or missed opportunities for eligible homebuyers.
3. Additional Documentation: Participating in a DPA program may require borrowers to provide additional documentation, undergo additional underwriting scrutiny, or complete additional paperwork, which can extend the homebuying process and add complexity.
4. Impact on Loan Terms: Some DPA programs may restrict the types of mortgage loans or financing options available to borrowers, potentially limiting their ability to choose the most suitable loan product for their needs.
5. Potential Repayment Obligations: DPA loans or deferred payment assistance may come with repayment obligations or restrictions, requiring borrowers to repay all or a portion of the assistance provided over time, which could affect their long-term financial obligations.

Best Suited For: DPA programs are best suited for first-time homebuyers, low- and moderate-income individuals and families, and other eligible borrowers who may struggle to afford a down payment on a home without assistance. These programs are particularly beneficial for individuals who meet the income and credit requirements but lack the financial resources to cover upfront homeownership costs.

Realtor Guidance: Realtors play a crucial role in informing homebuyers about available DPA programs, explaining eligibility requirements and application processes, and connecting them with participating lenders and housing agencies. Realtors can help clients explore DPA options that align with their financial circumstances and homeownership goals, ensuring they make informed decisions about financing their home purchase. Additionally, realtors can collaborate with mortgage professionals and DPA program administrators to streamline the homebuying process and maximize opportunities for eligible buyers to secure down payment assistance. By staying informed about DPA program updates and requirements, realtors can empower their clients to navigate the complexities of homeownership financing and achieve their dreams of buying a home.

DPA Programs Across the US

1. **Regional Variations:** Down Payment Assistance (DPA) programs vary significantly across the United States, with each state, county, and city offering its own unique set of programs tailored to local housing markets, demographic needs, and funding resources. While some DPA programs are administered at the federal level and available nationwide, many programs are region-specific and designed to address local affordability challenges and housing priorities.

2. **Program Types:** DPA programs encompass a diverse range of initiatives aimed at assisting homebuyers with down payment and closing cost expenses. These programs may include grants, forgivable loans, deferred-payment loans, or second mortgages, providing financial assistance to eligible homebuyers based on income, household size, credit history, and other qualifying criteria. Additionally, DPA programs may target specific populations, such as first-time homebuyers, low-to-moderate-income households, veterans, teachers, or public service employees, to address unique housing needs and promote homeownership opportunities.

3. **Funding Sources:** DPA programs receive funding from various sources, including federal, state, and local government agencies, nonprofit organizations, housing authorities, community development funds, and private sector partnerships. Funding may be allocated through government grants, bond programs, tax credits, or philanthropic contributions, enabling DPA programs to provide financial assistance to eligible homebuyers and stimulate housing affordability and access to homeownership.

Realtor Access to Information:

91

1. **Online Resources:** Realtors can access information about DPA programs through online resources, including government websites, housing authority portals, and nonprofit organizations dedicated to affordable housing. These platforms typically provide detailed program descriptions, eligibility requirements, application procedures, and contact information for participating agencies or lenders, allowing realtors to research available DPA options and assist clients in navigating the application process.

2. **Local Housing Authorities:** Realtors can also reach out to local housing authorities, community development agencies, or homeownership counseling organizations in their area to inquire about DPA programs and eligibility criteria. Housing professionals and counselors can provide valuable insights into available resources, program availability, and assistance options tailored to specific homebuyer needs and preferences.

3. **Lender Partnerships:** Establishing partnerships with mortgage lenders familiar with DPA programs can be beneficial for realtors seeking information and assistance for their clients. Lenders specializing in affordable housing loans often have expertise in DPA program requirements, application procedures, and documentation, allowing realtors to collaborate with knowledgeable professionals to facilitate DPA financing for eligible homebuyers.

4. **Networking and Training Events:** Realtors can stay informed about DPA programs by attending networking events, industry conferences, or training workshops hosted by local real estate associations, housing organizations, or government agencies. These events may feature presentations, panel discussions, or educational sessions on DPA initiatives, funding opportunities, and best practices for realtors assisting clients with DPA financing.

Talking Points for Realtors

1. **Program Diversity:** Highlight the diversity of DPA programs available across the US, ranging from federal initiatives to

localized efforts addressing specific housing needs and demographic groups.

2. **Accessibility:** Emphasize the accessibility of DPA program information through online resources, local housing authorities, lender partnerships, and networking events, enabling realtors to connect clients with available assistance options.

3. **Client Education:** Encourage realtors to educate clients about DPA programs, eligibility requirements, and benefits, empowering homebuyers to explore financing options and maximize affordability in their home purchase journey.

4. **Collaboration:** Advocate for collaboration between realtors, lenders, housing professionals, and community stakeholders to promote awareness of DPA programs, facilitate access to resources, and expand homeownership opportunities for underserved populations.

5. **Continued Learning:** Encourage realtors to stay informed about evolving DPA programs, policy changes, and funding opportunities through ongoing education, training, and professional development, ensuring they remain well-equipped to assist clients with DPA financing now and in the future.

Factors to Consider When Selecting the Right Loan

Selecting the right loan program is a critical decision in the home buying process, as it directly impacts a buyer's financial stability and long-term homeownership success. Several key factors must be considered to ensure that the chosen loan program aligns with the client's financial goals, lifestyle, and future plans. In this section, we will explore the essential factors to consider when selecting a loan program for clients, with a focus on how realtors can effectively communicate this information to home buyers.

1. **Financial Situation:** The client's financial situation is a fundamental factor in determining the appropriate loan program. Realtors should assess their clients' income, savings, credit history, debt obligations, and overall financial stability to understand their borrowing capacity and affordability. Different loan programs have varying requirements and eligibility criteria based on these financial factors, making it crucial for realtors to guide clients in evaluating their financial readiness.

2. **Long-Term Goals:** Understanding the client's long-term homeownership goals is essential in selecting the right loan program. Some clients may prioritize lower monthly payments and long-term stability, making fixed-rate mortgages a suitable option. Others may prefer flexibility and lower initial payments, making adjustable-rate mortgages or FHA loans more appealing. Realtors should discuss the client's future plans, such as potential job changes, family growth, or relocation, to ensure that the chosen loan program aligns with their evolving needs.

3. **Risk Tolerance:** Assessing the client's risk tolerance is crucial in choosing the appropriate loan program. Some clients may prefer the certainty and stability of fixed-rate mortgages, while others may be comfortable with the potential fluctuations of adjustable-rate mortgages in exchange for lower initial payments. Realtors should educate clients about the potential risks and benefits of each loan program and help them make informed decisions based on their risk tolerance and financial objectives.

4. **Property Type and Location:** The type and location of the property can influence the selection of the loan program. Certain loan programs, such as FHA loans or USDA loans, have specific eligibility requirements based on the property type and location. Realtors should consider the client's desired property type (e.g., single-family home, condominium, multi-family property) and location preferences when recommending loan programs to ensure compatibility with the chosen property.

5. **Closing Timeline:** The client's desired closing timeline is another factor to consider when selecting a loan program. Some

loan programs may offer faster approval and closing processes, making them suitable for clients with urgent timelines or competitive real estate markets. Realtors should discuss the client's timeline constraints and work with lenders to identify loan programs that can accommodate their closing needs effectively.

6. **Down Payment Options:** Different loan programs offer varying down payment requirements, ranging from 0% down for VA loans to conventional loans requiring a minimum down payment of 3% to 20%. Realtors should assess the client's down payment capabilities and preferences and explore loan programs that offer suitable down payment options. Additionally, realtors can educate clients about down payment assistance programs and grant opportunities to help bridge affordability gaps.

7. **Interest Rate and Terms:** Comparing interest rates, loan terms, and overall loan costs is essential in selecting the right loan program. Realtors should work closely with lenders to obtain loan estimates and analyze the projected monthly payments, total interest costs, and potential savings over the loan term. By helping clients understand the implications of different interest rates and loan terms, realtors empower them to make informed decisions that align with their financial objectives.

Realtor's Guidance: Realtors play a crucial role in guiding clients through the loan selection process and facilitating informed decision-making. By understanding the client's financial situation, long-term goals, risk tolerance, property preferences, closing timeline, down payment options, and interest rate considerations, realtors can effectively recommend loan programs that meet their unique needs and priorities. Realtors should communicate openly and transparently with clients, providing educational resources, loan comparisons, and expert guidance to empower them to navigate the complexities of mortgage financing confidently.

Selecting the right loan program is a collaborative effort between realtors, clients, and lenders, requiring careful consideration of various factors to ensure a successful and sustainable homeownership experience. By understanding the key factors to consider when selecting a loan program and effectively communicating this information to home buyers, realtors can empower clients to make informed decisions that align with their financial goals and lifestyle preferences. Through proactive engagement, personalized guidance, and comprehensive support, realtors can help clients navigate the loan selection process with confidence and achieve their dream of homeownership.

As we conclude Chapter 5, we reflect on the enlightening journey through the diverse landscape of mortgage loan programs and options. This chapter has been a beacon of knowledge, illuminating the myriad pathways available to both realtors and homebuyers in their pursuit of homeownership dreams.

Mortgage loan programs stand as pillars of support, offering a multitude of options tailored to meet the unique needs and circumstances of borrowers. From conventional loans to government-backed programs, each avenue presents its own set of advantages and considerations, empowering realtors to guide their clients towards the most suitable financing solutions.

Through comprehensive exploration and analysis, realtors have equipped themselves with the expertise to navigate the intricacies of mortgage loan programs. Armed with this knowledge, they serve as trusted advisors, steering their clients towards programs that align with their financial goals, preferences, and eligibility criteria.

In the ever-evolving landscape of real estate financing, education emerges as a powerful tool, empowering both realtors and homebuyers to make informed decisions. By demystifying the complexities of mortgage loan programs and options, realtors foster confidence and clarity, paving the way for successful home purchases and fulfilling homeownership experiences.

As we bid farewell to Chapter 5, let us carry forth the insights gained and lessons learned. Realtors emerge as architects of opportunity, guiding their clients towards mortgage loan programs that lay the foundation for their future homes. With knowledge as their compass and expertise as their guide, realtors and homebuyers embark on their journey with assurance and optimism, poised to transform dreams into reality in the vibrant tapestry of real estate.

Chapter 7

Mortgage Rates and Interest

In the dynamic landscape of real estate, understanding mortgage rates and interest is paramount for both realtors and home buyers alike. Chapter 6 delves into the intricate world of mortgage rates and interest, offering invaluable insights to navigate this fundamental aspect of the home buying process.

Mortgage rates, often referred to as the cost of borrowing money, play a pivotal role in determining the affordability and feasibility of homeownership. In this chapter, we will explore the factors influencing mortgage rates, including economic indicators, market trends, and lender policies. By gaining a comprehensive understanding of mortgage rates, realtors can empower their clients to make informed decisions regarding loan selection and financial planning.

Mortgage rates directly impact home buying decisions, influencing the overall affordability of properties and the monthly mortgage payments. As mortgage rates fluctuate in response to economic conditions and market dynamics, realtors must stay abreast of the latest trends and developments to provide accurate guidance and recommendations to their clients. By leveraging their knowledge of mortgage rates, realtors can help clients capitalize on favorable market conditions and secure competitive financing options.

Effective communication is key when discussing mortgage rates and interest with home buyers. In this chapter, we will explore communication strategies and techniques that realtors can employ to educate and inform their clients about mortgage rates, interest rate trends, and their implications for the home buying process. From breaking down complex financial concepts to providing personalized insights tailored to individual client needs, realtors can enhance client understanding and confidence in navigating the intricacies of mortgage financing.

Ultimately, the goal of understanding mortgage rates and interest is to empower home buyers to make informed and confident decisions throughout the home buying journey. By equipping realtors with the knowledge and tools necessary to navigate mortgage rates and interest effectively, this chapter aims to enhance client satisfaction, facilitate smoother transactions, and foster long-term relationships built on trust and expertise.

This Chapter serves as a comprehensive guide to understanding mortgage rates and interest, offering practical insights and actionable strategies for realtors to leverage in their client interactions. By mastering the nuances of mortgage rates and interest, realtors can enhance their value proposition, elevate the client experience, and drive positive outcomes in the ever-evolving real estate landscape.

Understanding Mortgage Rates

Mortgage rates, the interest rates charged on mortgage loans, are influenced by a myriad of interconnected factors that require a comprehensive understanding for effective decision-making in the home buying process. Let's delve deeper into each contributing factor to gain a thorough understanding of mortgage rate dynamics and their implications for realtors and home buyers.

Economic Indicators: Economic indicators serve as barometers of the economy's health and play a crucial role in shaping mortgage rates. Key indicators include:

> **GDP Growth:** Robust economic growth typically leads to higher mortgage rates as demand for loans increases, driving borrowing costs upward.

- **Inflation Rates:** Inflation erodes the purchasing power of currency, prompting central banks to raise interest rates to curb inflation. Consequently, mortgage rates rise to reflect higher borrowing costs.
- **Employment Figures:** Low unemployment rates and strong job creation signal a healthy economy, leading to increased consumer spending and borrowing, which can drive up mortgage rates.

Central Bank Policies: Central banks, such as the Federal Reserve in the United States, wield significant influence over mortgage rates through their monetary policy decisions. Key policy tools include:

- **Interest Rate Adjustments:** Central banks set benchmark interest rates, such as the federal funds rate in the U.S., which serve as a guide for other interest rates, including mortgage rates. When central banks raise interest rates to combat inflation or cool economic growth, mortgage rates tend to rise in tandem. Conversely, rate cuts stimulate borrowing and may lead to lower mortgage rates.

Supply and Demand Dynamics: The supply and demand for mortgage-backed securities (MBS) impact mortgage rates by affecting the availability of funds for lending. Key considerations include:

- **Investor Appetite:** Investors' demand for MBS, which are bundles of mortgages sold to investors, influences mortgage rates. High demand for MBS can lead to lower mortgage rates as lenders offer competitive rates to attract investors seeking higher returns.

- **Market Conditions:** Market sentiment, economic outlook, and regulatory changes can also influence demand for MBS, thereby affecting mortgage rates. Economic uncertainty or regulatory changes may lead to increased risk perception among investors, resulting in higher mortgage rates.

Credit Risk: Individual borrower characteristics, such as credit score, debt-to-income ratio, and down payment size, play a significant role in determining mortgage rates for individual borrowers. Key considerations include:

- **Credit Score:** A higher credit score indicates lower credit risk to lenders, leading to lower mortgage rates. Conversely, borrowers with lower credit scores may face higher rates to offset the increased risk of default.

- As you guide your clients through the process of searching for their dream home, it's crucial to ensure they understand the significant role their credit score plays in securing a mortgage. Here's how you can assist them in navigating this aspect of the homebuying journey:

- **Education is Key:** Many clients may not fully grasp how their credit score impacts their ability to obtain a mortgage and the terms they'll receive. Take the time to educate them about the importance of maintaining a good credit score and how it directly affects their loan eligibility and interest rates.

- **Assess their Credit Profile:** Encourage your clients to obtain a copy of their credit report and review it for accuracy. Help them understand the factors that influence their score and suggest strategies for improvement, such as paying down debt and correcting errors.

- **Prepare for Mortgage Approval:** By understanding your clients' credit profiles, you can help them anticipate the type of mortgage products they may qualify for and the potential interest rates they could secure. This information empowers them to take proactive steps to improve their credit scores before applying for a mortgage.

- **Connect with Reputable Lenders:** Leverage your network of mortgage lenders to connect your clients with reputable professionals who can assist them in securing financing. Facilitate introductions between clients and lenders, ensuring they have access to the expertise they need throughout the mortgage application process.

- **Negotiation Support:** Highlight the strength of your clients' creditworthiness during negotiations with sellers. A strong credit profile can give them leverage and potentially influence the negotiation process in their favor, particularly in competitive markets.

- **Long-Term Financial Planning:** Emphasize the importance of maintaining good credit habits even after purchasing a home. Help your clients understand how their credit score impacts their overall financial health and future borrowing opportunities.

By guiding your clients through the intricacies of credit scores and mortgage financing, you play a crucial role in helping them achieve their homeownership goals while securing the best possible terms for their investment. Your expertise and support are invaluable assets as they embark on this exciting journey.

Getting a Credit Report

As a realtor, you can guide your clients through the process of obtaining a copy of their credit report by suggesting the following steps:

1. **Direct Them to AnnualCreditReport.com:** This is the only website authorized by the federal government to provide free credit reports from the three major credit bureaus – Equifax, Experian, and TransUnion. Encourage your clients to visit this website to request their reports online.

2. **Explain the Annual Free Credit Report:** Inform your clients that they are entitled to one free credit report from each of the three credit bureaus every 12 months. Remind them that they should stagger their requests to review their reports from each bureau throughout the year for a comprehensive overview of their credit history.

3. **Provide Paper Request Forms:** Some clients may prefer to request their credit reports by mail. You can provide them with paper request forms available on AnnualCreditReport.com, which they can print out, fill in, and mail to the designated addresses of the credit bureaus.

4. **Discuss Credit Monitoring Services:** While not necessary for obtaining a free credit report, you can discuss the option of signing up for credit monitoring services with your clients. These services provide ongoing access to credit reports and alerts for any changes or suspicious activity. However, they typically involve a subscription fee.

5. **Advise on Reviewing and Disputing Errors:** Once your clients receive their credit reports, advise them to carefully review the information for accuracy. If they find any errors or discrepancies, encourage them to follow the credit bureau's dispute process to have the information corrected.

6. **Offer Guidance for Interpretation:** Explain to your clients how to interpret the information on their credit reports,

including understanding their credit score, payment history, credit utilization, and any negative marks such as late payments or collections. Offer assistance in interpreting any complex or confusing details.

7. By guiding your clients through the process of obtaining and understanding their credit reports, you empower them to take control of their financial health and make informed decisions as they navigate the homebuying process. This demonstrates your commitment to their success and builds trust in your role as their trusted advisor.

Debt-to-Income Ratio

The debt-to-income (DTI) ratio is a crucial financial metric used by lenders to assess a borrower's ability to manage their debt obligations in relation to their income. It's a measure of how much of a person's monthly income is allocated towards debt repayment, and it's expressed as a percentage.

Here's How to Calculate the Debt-to-Income Ratio

1. **Calculate Monthly Debt Payments:** Start by adding up all of your monthly debt payments. This typically includes mortgage or rent payments, car loans, student loans, credit card minimum payments, and any other monthly debt obligations.

2. **Calculate Monthly Gross Income:** Determine your total gross monthly income before taxes and deductions. This can include income from salaries, wages, bonuses, commissions, rental income, and any other regular sources of income.

3. **Divide Debt Payments by Gross Income:** Divide your total monthly debt payments by your gross monthly income, then multiply the result by 100 to convert it into a percentage.

The formula for calculating the debt-to-income ratio is

$$DTI\ Ratio = (\frac{Total\ Monthly\ Debt\ Payments}{Gross\ Monthly\ Income}) \times 100$$

For example, if your total monthly debt payments are $2,000 and your gross monthly income is $6,000, your DTI ratio would be:

$$DTI\ Ratio = (\frac{2,000}{6,000}) \times 100 = 33.33\%$$

Once you've calculated the DTI ratio, here's how realtors can coach their clients when buying a home:

Understanding DTI Requirements

Educate your clients about the importance of DTI ratios in the mortgage approval process. Different lenders may have varying DTI ratio requirements, but typically, a lower DTI ratio is preferred as it indicates a borrower's ability to manage additional debt.

1. **Assessing Affordability:** Help your clients assess their financial situation by calculating their DTI ratio. By comparing their existing debt obligations to their income, they can determine how much additional debt they can comfortably take on for a mortgage payment without overextending themselves financially.

2. **Setting Realistic Budgets:** Based on your clients' DTI ratio and lender requirements, assist them in setting a realistic budget for their home purchase. This ensures that they focus on properties within their financial means and avoid the risk of being house poor.

3. **Improving DTI Ratio:** If your clients have a high DTI ratio, work with them to explore strategies for improving it before applying for a mortgage. This may include paying down existing debt, increasing income, or considering debt consolidation options.

4. **Selecting Mortgage Products:** Recommend mortgage products that align with your clients' DTI ratio and financial goals. Some mortgage programs may have more flexible DTI ratio requirements, which can be beneficial for clients with higher ratios.

5. **Negotiating Terms:** Highlight the importance of a strong financial profile, including a low DTI ratio, during negotiations with sellers. A lower DTI ratio can signal financial stability to sellers and strengthen your clients' offers in competitive markets.

By coaching your clients on understanding and managing their DTI ratio, you empower them to make informed decisions throughout the homebuying process. This guidance not only helps them secure mortgage approval but also sets them on a path toward long-term financial success as homeowners.

Down Payment Size

The down payment size refers to the initial payment made by the homebuyer towards the purchase price of the home. It's typically expressed as a percentage of the total purchase price, and it plays a significant role in the homebuying process.

Here's How to Calculate the Down Payment Size

4. **Determine the Purchase Price:** Start by identifying the total purchase price of the home. This is the amount agreed upon between the buyer and seller.

5. **Decide on the Down Payment Percentage:** The down payment percentage can vary depending on factors such as loan type, lender requirements, and personal financial circumstances. Common down payment percentages range from 3% to 20% or more of the purchase price.

6. **Calculate the Down Payment Amount:** Multiply the purchase price of the home by the chosen down payment percentage to determine the down payment amount.

> For example, if the purchase price of the home is $300,000 and the down payment percentage is 20%, the down payment amount would be:
>
> Down Payment Amount = Purchase Price × Down Payment Percentage
>
> Down Payment Amount = $300,000 × 0.20 = $60,000

Once you've calculated the down payment size, here's how realtors can coach their clients when buying a home:

7. **Understanding Down Payment Requirements:** Educate your clients about the importance of the down payment in the homebuying process. Explain how the down payment size affects the loan-to-value (LTV) ratio and influences mortgage terms and interest rates.

8. **Assessing Financial Capacity:** Help your clients evaluate their financial situation to determine an appropriate down payment size. Consider factors such as available savings, budget constraints, and long-term financial goals when discussing down payment options.

9. **Exploring Down Payment Assistance Programs:** Inform your clients about potential down payment assistance programs available to first-time homebuyers, low-income households, and other eligible individuals. These programs can help reduce the upfront cost of homeownership and make homeownership more accessible.

10. **Comparing Mortgage Options:** Discuss various mortgage options with your clients and how different down payment sizes impact loan terms and monthly payments. Help them weigh the

pros and cons of different down payment percentages and mortgage products to make an informed decision.

11. **Planning for Closing Costs:** Remind your clients to budget for closing costs in addition to the down payment. Closing costs typically include fees for loan origination, appraisal, title insurance, and other expenses associated with the home purchase.

12. **Negotiating Terms:** Emphasize the benefits of a larger down payment, such as reducing the loan-to-value ratio and potentially qualifying for lower mortgage rates. Use this leverage during negotiations with sellers to strengthen your clients' offers and improve their chances of securing their desired property.

By coaching your clients on understanding and strategizing their down payment size, you help them navigate the homebuying process with confidence and achieve their homeownership goals effectively. This personalized guidance ensures that your clients make informed decisions that align with their financial capabilities and long-term objectives.

Basis Points and Buy-Downs

Understanding Basis Points: A basis point (abbreviated as "bps") is a unit of measure commonly used in finance to denote changes in interest rates, yields, and other financial percentages. One basis point is equal to 0.01%, or one one-hundredth of a percentage point. For example, if an interest rate increases from 3.75% to 3.76%, it has risen by one basis point. Basis points are particularly useful when discussing changes in interest rates or yields on financial instruments, such as bonds, loans, or mortgages. They provide a precise and standardized way to express these changes, especially when dealing with small percentage movements.

Buying Down an Interest Rate: Buying down an interest rate involves paying an upfront fee to the lender in exchange for a lower interest rate on a mortgage loan. This process is also known as "discount points" or "mortgage points." Each point typically costs 1% of the total loan amount and typically lowers the interest rate by a certain number of basis points, usually 25 basis points (0.25%).

For example, if a borrower is offered a 30-year fixed-rate mortgage with an interest rate of 4.00%, they may have the option to "buy down" the rate by paying one discount point (1% of the loan amount). This could lower the interest rate to 3.75%.

How Realtors Can Coach Their Clients

Explaining Financial Concepts: Realtors can educate their clients about financial concepts such as basis points and buying down interest rates. By explaining these terms in simple, understandable language, realtors empower their clients to make informed decisions about mortgage options and financing strategies.

Assessing Affordability: Realtors can help clients assess their financial situation and determine how different interest rates and mortgage terms will impact their monthly payments and overall affordability. By considering factors such as income, debt, and budget constraints, realtors guide clients in selecting mortgage options that align with their financial goals.

Comparing Mortgage Offers: Realtors assist clients in comparing mortgage offers from different lenders, taking into account interest rates, discount points, and other terms and fees. By analyzing the long-term costs and benefits of each option, realtors help clients identify the most favorable mortgage for their needs.

Negotiating with Lenders: Realtors can negotiate with lenders on behalf of their clients to secure competitive interest rates and favorable mortgage terms. By leveraging their relationships with lenders and advocating for their clients' best interests, realtors ensure that clients receive the most advantageous financing options available.

Budgeting for Closing Costs: Realtors advise clients on budgeting for closing costs, including any fees associated with buying down the interest rate. By helping clients understand the total costs of homeownership, including upfront expenses, realtors ensure that clients are financially prepared for the homebuying process.

Long-Term Financial Planning: Realtors provide guidance on long-term financial planning, including strategies for building home equity and maximizing the benefits of homeownership. By helping clients understand the financial implications of their mortgage decisions, realtors support their clients' long-term financial success and homeownership goals.

Overall, by coaching their clients on financial concepts, assessing affordability, comparing mortgage offers, negotiating with lenders, budgeting for closing costs, and providing guidance on long-term financial planning, realtors play a critical role in helping clients navigate the homebuying process with confidence and achieve their homeownership goals effectively.

Lender Credits

A lender credit is a financial incentive provided by a lender to a borrower to offset some or all of the closing costs associated with obtaining a mortgage loan. This credit is typically offered as an alternative to the borrower paying discount points upfront to lower their interest rate. Instead of reducing the interest rate, the lender credits a certain amount towards the borrower's closing costs, effectively reducing the amount of cash the borrower needs to bring to the closing table.

Lender credits are often negotiated between the borrower and the lender during the mortgage application process. The amount of the credit can vary depending on factors such as the loan amount, interest rate, and the specific terms of the mortgage agreement. In some cases, borrowers may have the option to choose between receiving a lender credit or paying discount points to buy down their interest rate, depending on their financial goals and preferences.

Now, let's explore how realtors can coach their clients when buying a home, including understanding and leveraging lender credits:

Educating Clients on Mortgage Options

1. Realtors can educate their clients about the various mortgage options available to them, including the possibility of receiving a lender credit. By explaining the concept of lender credits and how they can help offset closing costs, realtors empower their

clients to make informed decisions about financing their home purchase.

2. **Assessing Financial Needs:** Realtors work with their clients to assess their financial situation and determine the most appropriate mortgage strategy based on their budget, cash reserves, and long-term financial goals. By understanding their clients' needs and priorities, realtors can help them explore options for minimizing out-of-pocket expenses at closing, including leveraging lender credits.

3. **Negotiating with Lenders:** Realtors can negotiate with lenders on behalf of their clients to secure favorable terms, including lender credits. By leveraging their relationships with lenders and advocating for their clients' best interests, realtors can help clients maximize their financial benefits and minimize their upfront costs when obtaining a mortgage loan.

4. **Comparing Mortgage Offers:** Realtors assist clients in comparing mortgage offers from different lenders, taking into account interest rates, closing costs, and the availability of lender credits. By analyzing the total cost of borrowing and evaluating the impact of lender credits on the overall affordability of the loan, realtors help clients identify the most advantageous financing option for their needs.

5. **Budgeting for Closing Costs:** Realtors advise clients on budgeting for closing costs, including any fees associated with obtaining a mortgage loan. By helping clients understand the potential costs involved in the homebuying process and exploring options for reducing these expenses, realtors ensure that clients are financially prepared for the transaction.

6. **Long-Term Financial Planning:** Realtors provide guidance on long-term financial planning, including strategies for managing debt, building equity, and maximizing the benefits of homeownership. By helping clients understand the financial implications of their mortgage decisions, including the use of

lender credits, realtors support their clients' long-term financial success and homeownership goals.

7. Overall, by coaching their clients on mortgage options, assessing financial needs, negotiating with lenders, comparing mortgage offers, budgeting for closing costs, and providing guidance on long-term financial planning, realtors play a critical role in helping clients navigate the homebuying process with confidence and achieve their homeownership goals effectively.

8. **Utilizing Information as a Realtor:** Realtors play a pivotal role in guiding home buyers through the mortgage process by leveraging their understanding of interest rate determinants. By educating clients about economic indicators, central bank policies, and supply and demand dynamics, realtors empower them to anticipate rate changes and make informed decisions. Additionally, realtors can offer guidance on improving creditworthiness to qualify for favorable rates, ultimately facilitating successful home purchases.

    ✓   By comprehensively analyzing each contributing factor to mortgage rate determination, realtors and home buyers can navigate the complexities of the mortgage market with confidence, ensuring optimal financing solutions tailored to their needs and goals.

Strategies for Securing the Best Mortgage Interest Rates

Securing the best possible interest rates on a mortgage is a top priority for home buyers, as it can significantly impact the affordability of homeownership over the long term. To help clients achieve this goal, realtors can employ various strategies and provide valuable guidance throughout the home buying process. Let's explore these strategies in detail, with an emphasis on how realtors can effectively communicate and implement them to benefit their clients.

1. Improve Creditworthiness: A strong credit profile is essential for securing favorable mortgage rates. Realtors can advise clients to take proactive steps to improve their creditworthiness, such as:

- **Check Credit Reports:** Encourage clients to obtain copies of their credit reports from major credit bureaus and review them for inaccuracies or discrepancies.

- **Pay Down Debts:** Recommend paying down outstanding debts to lower the debt-to-income ratio and improve credit utilization, both of which can positively impact credit scores.

- **Avoid Opening New Accounts:** Advise clients against opening new lines of credit or taking on additional debt, as this can temporarily lower credit scores and affect mortgage eligibility.

2. Save for a Larger Down Payment: A larger down payment not only reduces the loan amount but also demonstrates financial stability to lenders, potentially leading to lower interest rates. Realtors can suggest the following strategies to help clients save for a substantial down payment:

- **Set Savings Goals:** Assist clients in setting realistic savings goals and creating a budget to allocate funds toward their down payment.

- **Explore Down Payment Assistance Programs:** Educate clients about down payment assistance programs offered by government agencies, nonprofits, or employers, which can help bridge the gap between savings and the required down payment.

- **Consider Delaying the Home Purchase:** Encourage clients to postpone their home purchase to save more for a larger down payment, potentially qualifying for better rates and terms in the future.

3. Shop Around for Lenders: Not all lenders offer the same mortgage rates and terms, making it essential for home buyers to compare offers from multiple lenders. Realtors can guide clients through the lender selection process by:

- **Researching Lenders:** Research reputable lenders in the area and provide clients with a list of options to consider.

- **Requesting Multiple Quotes:** Encourage clients to obtain mortgage quotes from several lenders and compare the interest rates, closing costs, and terms offered.

- **Negotiating with Lenders:** Realtors can leverage their negotiation skills to advocate for competitive rates and terms on behalf of their clients, potentially securing better offers from lenders.

4. Consider Adjustable-Rate Mortgages (ARMs) or Hybrid ARMs: For clients planning to stay in their home for a relatively short period or expecting changes in their financial situation, adjustable-rate mortgages (ARMs) or hybrid ARMs may offer lower initial interest rates compared to fixed-rate mortgages. Realtors can help clients evaluate the pros and cons of ARMs, including:

- **Understanding Rate Adjustment Terms:** Educate clients about how ARMs work, including the initial fixed-rate period, adjustment frequency, and rate caps to mitigate potential risks.

- **Assessing Long-Term Financial Plans:** Discuss clients' long-term financial goals and assess whether an ARM aligns with their plans and risk tolerance.

- **Monitoring Market Trends:** Stay informed about interest rate trends and economic indicators to provide clients with timely advice on when to lock in a fixed rate or refinance an ARM if necessary.

5. Timing the Market: Mortgage interest rates fluctuate based on various economic factors and market conditions. Realtors can help clients capitalize on favorable rate environments by:

- **Monitoring Interest Rate Trends:** Stay informed about current interest rates and market forecasts to advise clients on when to lock in a rate or proceed with their home purchase.

- **Consider Rate Locks:** Educate clients about rate lock options offered by lenders, allowing them to secure a specific interest rate for a set period, protecting against potential rate increases during the home buying process.

- **Anticipating Economic Events:** Advise clients to consider economic events, such as Federal Reserve announcements or major economic reports, which can impact mortgage rates and inform their decision-making process.

Utilizing Information as a Realtor: Realtors play a pivotal role in guiding clients through the process of securing the best possible interest rates on their mortgages. By providing personalized advice, facilitating lender comparisons, and staying abreast of market trends, realtors can empower clients to make informed decisions that align with their financial goals and preferences. Ultimately, by employing these strategies, realtors can enhance the home buying experience for their clients and help them achieve their homeownership dreams with confidence.

As we conclude Chapter 7, we've journeyed through the intricate landscape of mortgage rates and interest, unraveling the complexities that underpin this fundamental aspect of the real estate world. From understanding the factors influencing mortgage rates to strategizing ways to secure the best possible interest rates, this chapter has equipped both realtors and home buyers with invaluable insights and actionable strategies.

Mortgage rates, often likened to the heartbeat of the real estate market, pulsate in response to a myriad of economic indicators, central bank policies, and supply and demand dynamics. Realtors, armed with this knowledge, stand as beacons of guidance, navigating their clients through the ebb and flow of interest rate fluctuations.

Communication emerges as a cornerstone in the dialogue between realtors and home buyers, with effective communication strategies serving as bridges to understanding complex financial concepts. By breaking down the intricacies of mortgage rates and interest, realtors empower their clients to make informed decisions, paving the path towards homeownership with confidence.

From decoding credit scores to evaluating debt-to-income ratios and navigating the nuances of down payment size, realtors serve as trusted advisors, guiding their clients towards financial prosperity. By leveraging lender credits, exploring mortgage options, and negotiating with lenders, realtors orchestrate symphonies of success in the realm of real estate financing.

As we part ways with Chapter 7, let us carry forth the wisdom gleaned from our exploration of mortgage rates and interest. Armed with knowledge and guided by expertise, realtors and home buyers alike embark on their respective journeys with newfound confidence and clarity, poised to conquer the ever-evolving landscape of real estate with resilience and resolve.

Handling Mortgage Challenges and Pitfalls

Navigating the mortgage process can be complex and fraught with potential challenges and pitfalls for home buyers. From credit issues to documentation requirements, various factors can impact the smooth progression of a mortgage application. In Chapter 8, we dive into the intricacies of handling these challenges and pitfalls, providing realtors with valuable insights and strategies to support their clients through the mortgage journey.

The mortgage landscape is replete with potential challenges and pitfalls that can arise at any stage of the application process. From credit issues and income verification to appraisal discrepancies and loan denials, home buyers may encounter numerous hurdles along the way. Realtors play a crucial role in helping clients anticipate and navigate these challenges effectively, ensuring a successful outcome.

Chapter 8 equips realtors with the knowledge and strategies needed to address common mortgage challenges and pitfalls head-on. By understanding the root causes of these issues and implementing proactive measures, realtors can mitigate risks and guide their clients toward favorable solutions. From proactive credit management to effective communication with lenders, realtors will gain valuable insights into best practices for overcoming obstacles in the mortgage process.

Effective communication is paramount in addressing mortgage challenges and pitfalls. Realtors must be adept at conveying complex information in a clear and accessible manner, empowering clients to make informed decisions. By fostering open dialogue and providing ongoing support, realtors can alleviate concerns and instill confidence in their clients throughout the mortgage journey.

This serves as a comprehensive resource for realtors seeking to navigate the intricacies of mortgage challenges and pitfalls. By leveraging the knowledge and strategies outlined in this chapter, realtors can enhance their ability to support clients through the mortgage process effectively. From proactive problem-solving to empathetic communication, realtors will gain invaluable tools for guiding their clients toward successful homeownership despite potential obstacles along the way.

Navigating Common Mortgage Challenges and Setbacks

The journey to homeownership often involves navigating through a myriad of challenges and obstacles in the mortgage process. From credit issues to appraisal discrepancies, various factors can impede the smooth progression of a mortgage application. In this comprehensive guide, we'll explore some of the common challenges encountered in the mortgage process and provide strategies for overcoming them, with a focus on how realtors can effectively communicate and support home buyers through these hurdles.

1. Credit Challenges: Credit issues are among the most prevalent hurdles faced by home buyers during the mortgage process. Low credit scores, past bankruptcies, and high debt levels can hinder a borrower's ability to qualify for a mortgage or secure favorable interest rates. To overcome credit challenges, realtors can advise clients to review their credit reports, identify areas for improvement, and take steps to boost their credit scores. This may include paying off outstanding debts, disputing inaccuracies on credit reports, and establishing a history of timely payments.

2. Documentation Requirements: The mortgage process entails extensive documentation to verify income, assets, and other financial information. Missing or incomplete documentation can delay loan approval and frustrate both home buyers and lenders. Realtors can help clients anticipate documentation requirements by providing a comprehensive list of required documents and assisting them in gathering and organizing the necessary paperwork. By staying organized and proactive, home buyers can streamline the documentation process and expedite their mortgage application.

What's Needed

Proof of Income: Lenders typically require recent pay stubs, W-2 forms, and tax returns to verify income. Self-employed individuals may need to provide additional documentation, such as profit and loss statements or 1099 forms.

Asset Documentation: Borrowers need to provide statements from bank accounts, retirement accounts, and investment accounts to verify assets. These statements should typically cover the most recent two to three months.

Employment Verification: Lenders may request verification of employment directly from employers to confirm job status, income stability, and any recent changes in employment.

Credit History: Borrowers need to authorize the lender to pull their credit report, which contains information about their credit history, outstanding debts, and payment history.

Additional Documentation: Depending on the borrower's financial situation and the lender's requirements, additional documentation may be requested, such as rental history, divorce decrees, or explanations for any derogatory credit issues.

How Realtors Can Coach Their Clients

Educating Clients: Realtors should educate their clients about the importance of documentation in the mortgage process and the potential consequences of missing or incomplete paperwork. By explaining the role of each document and the significance of providing accurate information, realtors empower their clients to navigate the documentation process effectively.

Providing a Checklist: Realtors can provide clients with a comprehensive checklist of required documents based on the lender's requirements. This checklist serves as a roadmap for clients, helping them gather and organize the necessary paperwork in advance of their mortgage application.

Setting Expectations: Realtors should set clear expectations with their clients regarding the documentation process, including timelines and potential challenges. By preparing clients for what to expect, realtors help alleviate stress and minimize surprises during the mortgage application process.

Assisting with Organization: Realtors can assist clients in organizing their documentation by providing tips for keeping paperwork organized and easily accessible. This may include using digital tools, such as scanning documents or storing them securely online, to streamline the process.

Encouraging Proactivity: Realtors should encourage clients to be proactive in gathering and submitting documentation to the lender promptly. Emphasizing the importance of timely communication and follow-up helps clients stay on track and avoid delays in the mortgage approval process.

Offering Support: Throughout the documentation process, realtors should offer ongoing support and guidance to their clients, answering any questions they may have and addressing any concerns or challenges that arise. By being a trusted resource and advocate for their clients, realtors help ensure a smooth and successful mortgage application experience.

By coaching their clients on documentation requirements, providing a checklist of required documents, setting expectations, assisting with organization, encouraging proactivity, and offering ongoing support, realtors play a vital role in helping clients navigate the mortgage process with confidence and achieve their homeownership goals effectively.

3. Appraisal Discrepancies: Appraisal discrepancies, where the appraised value of the property differs from the agreed-upon purchase price, can pose challenges in the mortgage process. A low appraisal value may jeopardize loan approval or require renegotiation of the purchase price. Realtors can help clients navigate appraisal discrepancies by conducting thorough market research, providing comparable sales data to support the property's value, and advocating for a reassessment if necessary. By addressing appraisal issues proactively, realtors can help home buyers overcome this common challenge and move forward with their mortgage application.

4. Loan Denials: Despite meticulous preparation and documentation, some home buyers may face the disappointment of loan denial during the mortgage process. This can occur due to factors such as insufficient income, excessive debt, or changes in creditworthiness. When confronted with a loan denial, realtors can offer support and guidance to their clients by exploring alternative financing options, such as government-backed loans or private lenders. By leveraging their network and resources, realtors can help home buyers rebound from a loan denial and pursue alternative pathways to homeownership.

5. Communication Breakdowns: Effective communication is essential in navigating the mortgage process, yet breakdowns between home buyers, realtors, and lenders can occur. Misunderstandings, delays in response, and lack of clarity can exacerbate tensions and prolong the mortgage journey. Realtors can serve as facilitators of communication, ensuring that all parties are informed and engaged throughout the process. By maintaining open lines of communication, realtors can address concerns promptly, clarify expectations, and foster a collaborative approach to overcoming challenges in the mortgage process.

Navigating common challenges and setbacks in the mortgage process requires patience, perseverance, and proactive problem-solving. Realtors play a vital role in guiding home buyers through these hurdles, offering support, advocacy, and expertise every step of the way. By understanding common challenges and implementing proactive measures, realtors can empower their clients to achieve their dream of homeownership despite the obstacles they may encounter along the path.

Strategies for Ensuring a Smooth Transaction

The process of buying a home can be fraught with potential risks and setbacks, but with careful planning and proactive strategies, realtors can help their clients navigate these challenges and ensure a smooth transaction. In this segment, we'll explore effective strategies for mitigating risks and overcoming setbacks in the home buying process, with a focus on how realtors can leverage this information when communicating with home buyers.

1. Conduct Comprehensive Due Diligence: One of the most effective ways to mitigate risks in a real estate transaction is by conducting thorough due diligence. Realtors should encourage their clients to conduct inspections, review property disclosures, and investigate any potential issues that may arise during the transaction. By identifying potential risks early on, realtors can help their clients make informed decisions and avoid costly surprises later in the process.

2. Address Financing Contingencies: Financing contingencies are a common source of uncertainty in real estate transactions. Realtors should work closely with their clients to ensure that financing contingencies are properly addressed and that their clients have a clear understanding of their financial obligations. This may involve working with lenders to secure pre-approval or pre-qualification letters, ensuring that financing is in place before making an offer, and exploring alternative financing options if needed.

3. Communicate Effectively and Transparently: Communication is key to a successful real estate transaction. Realtors should maintain open lines of communication with their clients, keeping them informed of any developments and addressing any concerns or questions they may have promptly. By providing clear and transparent communication throughout the process, realtors can help alleviate anxiety and uncertainty and build trust with their clients.

4. Anticipate and Plan for Potential Setbacks: Despite careful planning, setbacks may still occur during the home buying process. Realtors should work with their clients to anticipate potential setbacks and develop contingency plans to address them. This may involve identifying alternative properties or financing options, negotiating with sellers to address issues that arise during inspections, or exploring creative solutions to overcome obstacles that may arise.

5. Leverage Professional Networks and Resources: Realtors should leverage their professional networks and resources to help their clients navigate potential risks and setbacks. This may involve working closely with lenders, inspectors, attorneys, and other professionals to address issues as they arise and ensure a smooth transaction. By tapping into their network of trusted professionals, realtors can provide their clients with access to expertise and resources that can help mitigate risks and overcome obstacles.

Mitigating risks and ensuring a smooth transaction in a real estate transaction requires careful planning, effective communication, and proactive problem-solving. Realtors play a crucial role in guiding their clients through the home buying process, offering support, expertise, and guidance every step of the way. By implementing these strategies and leveraging their knowledge and resources, realtors can help their clients navigate potential risks and setbacks and achieve a successful and stress-free transaction.

Chapter 8 has provided a comprehensive exploration of the challenges and pitfalls that home buyers may encounter in the mortgage process, offering valuable insights and strategies for realtors to support their clients through these hurdles effectively.

From credit challenges to appraisal discrepancies and loan denials, the mortgage journey can be rife with complexities and uncertainties. However, armed with a deep understanding of common challenges and proactive problem-solving strategies, realtors can guide their clients toward successful outcomes in their home buying journey.

Effective communication emerges as a cornerstone in addressing mortgage challenges and pitfalls. By fostering open dialogue, providing ongoing support, and empowering clients to make informed decisions, realtors can alleviate concerns and instill confidence in their clients throughout the mortgage process.

This chapter serves as a comprehensive resource for realtors seeking to navigate the intricacies of mortgage challenges and pitfalls, equipping them with the knowledge and strategies needed to overcome obstacles and ensure a smooth transaction for their clients.

As you apply the insights and strategies outlined in this chapter in your interactions with home buyers, remember that proactive problem-solving, effective communication, and leveraging professional networks are key to mitigating risks and navigating setbacks in the home buying process. By guiding your clients with expertise and empathy, you can help them achieve their dream of homeownership despite the challenges they may encounter along the way.

Chapter 9

Communicating Effectively with Loan Officers

In the complex landscape of real estate transactions, effective communication is paramount. Nowhere is this more evident than in the relationship between realtors and loan officers. Chapter 8 delves into the critical importance of communicating effectively with loan officers throughout the home buying process.

As real estate professionals, realtors serve as the bridge between home buyers and loan officers, facilitating the exchange of information and ensuring that the financing aspect of the transaction progresses smoothly. This chapter highlights the key principles and strategies for fostering strong communication and collaboration between realtors and loan officers to achieve optimal outcomes for their clients.

Effective communication with loan officers encompasses various facets, from conveying client needs and preferences to facilitating the exchange of pertinent documentation. By establishing clear lines of communication and maintaining open dialogue, realtors can streamline the loan application process, address potential challenges proactively, and ultimately enhance the overall home buying experience for their clients.

Chapter 9 explores practical tips and best practices for realtors to communicate effectively with loan officers, including strategies for establishing rapport, managing expectations, and navigating potential obstacles. By honing their communication skills and fostering productive relationships with loan officers, realtors can better advocate for their clients' interests and facilitate successful real estate transactions.

Through insightful guidance and actionable advice, this chapter equips realtors with the tools and knowledge they need to navigate the intricacies of communicating effectively with loan officers, ultimately empowering them to deliver exceptional service and support to their clients throughout the home buying journey.

Importance of Collaboration Between Realtors and Loan Officers

In the intricate world of real estate transactions, collaboration between realtors and loan officers is indispensable. This partnership lays the foundation for a seamless home buying experience, ensuring that clients navigate the complexities of financing with confidence and ease. Chapter 8 explores the significance of collaboration between these key stakeholders and offers insights into how realtors can leverage this partnership to mitigate setbacks and optimize outcomes for their clients.

1. **Streamlining the Process:** Collaborating effectively with loan officers streamlines the mortgage application process, minimizing delays and expediting approvals. Realtors play a pivotal role in facilitating communication between clients and loan officers, ensuring that all necessary documentation is provided promptly and accurately. By fostering open dialogue and proactive engagement, realtors can prevent potential bottlenecks and keep the transaction on track.

2. **Managing Expectations:** Effective collaboration enables realtors to manage client expectations and provide realistic guidance throughout the home buying journey. Loan officers possess invaluable insights into current market conditions, lending criteria, and potential challenges that may arise during the mortgage process. By working closely with loan officers, realtors can offer clients informed advice and prepare them for various scenarios, empowering them to make well-informed decisions.

3. **Problem Solving:** Collaboration between realtors and loan officers facilitates effective problem solving when unexpected challenges arise. Whether it's addressing appraisal discrepancies, resolving documentation issues, or navigating loan denials, realtors and loan officers can pool their expertise to identify solutions and mitigate setbacks. By leveraging their collective knowledge and resources, they can navigate obstacles more effectively and keep the transaction moving forward.

4. **Advocating for Clients:** Perhaps most importantly, collaboration between realtors and loan officers allows for effective advocacy on behalf of clients. Realtors serve as advocates for their clients' best interests, ensuring that their needs and preferences are communicated clearly to loan officers. By building strong

relationships with loan officers based on trust and mutual respect, realtors can negotiate favorable terms, secure competitive financing options, and ultimately deliver exceptional outcomes for their clients.

Incorporating Collaboration Into Client Communication:
Effective collaboration between realtors and loan officers begins with clear and proactive communication with clients. Realtors should emphasize the importance of working closely with loan officers to their clients from the outset of the home buying process. By educating clients about the role of loan officers and the benefits of collaboration, realtors can instill confidence and trust in the partnership.

Realtors should also encourage clients to maintain open lines of communication with both their realtor and loan officer throughout the transaction. Regular updates and progress reports from the loan officer can help alleviate concerns and keep clients informed about the status of their mortgage application. By fostering a collaborative mindset among clients, realtors can reinforce the importance of teamwork and collective problem solving in achieving their homeownership goals.

Collaboration between realtors and loan officers is essential for optimizing the home buying experience and overcoming setbacks that may arise along the way. By working together effectively, realtors and loan officers can streamline the mortgage process, manage client expectations, solve problems, and advocate for their clients' best interests. Through proactive communication and a shared commitment to excellence, this collaborative partnership empowers realtors to deliver unparalleled service and support to their clients, ensuring a successful and rewarding home buying journey.

Establishing and Maintaining Open Lines of Communication

Effective communication lies at the heart of successful real estate transactions, fostering trust, transparency, and collaboration between realtors and home buyers. Chapter 8 delves into the importance of establishing and maintaining open lines of communication and offers practical tips for realtors to navigate potential setbacks while communicating with their clients.

1. **Setting Expectations:** From the outset of the client relationship, realtors should set clear expectations regarding communication channels, frequency, and response times. By establishing mutually agreed-upon guidelines, realtors can ensure that clients feel informed and supported throughout the home buying process. Whether it's through email updates, phone calls, or in-person meetings, realtors should tailor their communication approach to meet the individual preferences and needs of their clients.

2. **Active Listening:** Effective communication is a two-way street, requiring realtors to listen attentively to their clients' concerns, questions, and preferences. By practicing active listening, realtors can demonstrate empathy and understanding, building rapport and trust with their clients. Realtors should encourage open dialogue and create a safe space for clients to voice their thoughts and feelings, fostering a collaborative partnership based on mutual respect and shared goals.

3. **Providing Regular Updates:** Consistent and timely communication is essential for keeping clients informed and engaged throughout the home buying journey. Realtors should provide regular updates on market developments, property listings, and progress updates on the transaction. Whether it's a quick email or a scheduled phone call, realtors should make a concerted effort to keep clients in the loop and address any concerns or questions promptly.

4. **Utilizing Technology:** In today's digital age, technology offers a myriad of tools and platforms to facilitate communication between realtors and clients. From real estate apps and messaging platforms to virtual tours and video calls, realtors can leverage technology to enhance the client experience and streamline communication. By embracing innovative solutions, realtors can meet clients where they are and cater to their preferences for convenient and efficient communication.

5. Managing Expectations: Transparent communication is key to managing client expectations and ensuring a smooth transaction. Realtors should be upfront and honest with their clients about potential challenges, setbacks, and timelines associated with the home buying process. By setting realistic expectations and

providing honest assessments, realtors can mitigate surprises and empower clients to make informed decisions.

Overcoming Setbacks Through Communication

Despite proactive efforts to establish open lines of communication, setbacks may still arise during the home buying process. Realtors should approach these challenges with a solution-oriented mindset, using effective communication strategies to navigate obstacles and maintain trust with their clients.

- **Transparency:** In the face of setbacks, realtors should maintain transparency and honesty with their clients, providing clear explanations and updates on the situation. By keeping clients informed about potential delays or issues, realtors can manage expectations and minimize frustration.

- **Problem-Solving:** Effective communication enables realtors to collaborate with clients and other stakeholders to identify solutions to setbacks. By fostering open dialogue and brainstorming creative solutions, realtors can navigate obstacles more effectively and keep the transaction moving forward.

- **Emotional Support:** Setbacks in the home buying process can be emotionally challenging for clients. Realtors should offer empathy, reassurance, and support to help clients navigate these difficult moments with confidence and resilience. By demonstrating empathy and understanding, realtors can strengthen their bond with clients and build trust and loyalty over time.

Establishing and maintaining open lines of communication is essential for fostering strong client relationships and navigating potential setbacks in the home buying process. By setting clear expectations, practicing active listening, providing regular updates, utilizing technology, and managing expectations, realtors can enhance the client experience and empower their clients to achieve their homeownership goals. Through effective communication and proactive problem-solving, realtors can build trust, instill confidence, and ultimately, deliver exceptional service to their clients.

Fostering a Productive Working Relationship

In the realm of real estate, establishing a productive working relationship between realtors and their clients is paramount for achieving successful outcomes in home transactions. Chapter 8 delves into the best practices for fostering such relationships, emphasizing how realtors can navigate potential setbacks while effectively communicating with home buyers.

1. **Building Trust:** Trust forms the foundation of any productive working relationship. Realtors should strive to build trust with their clients by demonstrating integrity, competence, and reliability in every interaction. By delivering on promises, providing accurate information, and acting in their clients' best interests, realtors can earn the trust and confidence of their clients, laying the groundwork for a collaborative partnership.

2. **Understanding Client Needs:** Effective communication begins with understanding the unique needs, preferences, and goals of each client. Realtors should take the time to listen attentively to their clients, asking probing questions to uncover their motivations, priorities, and concerns. By gaining a deep understanding of their clients' aspirations and challenges, realtors can tailor their communication approach and service delivery to meet their clients' specific needs.

3. **Setting Clear Expectations:** Clear communication is essential for setting expectations and avoiding misunderstandings or disappointments down the line. Realtors should clearly outline their role, responsibilities, and the scope of services they provide to their clients. Additionally, realtors should establish clear expectations regarding communication channels, response times, and next steps in the home buying process. By aligning expectations from the outset, realtors can foster a sense of transparency and accountability in their working relationship with clients.

4. **Maintaining Professionalism:** Professionalism is a cornerstone of effective communication and relationship-building in real estate. Realtors should conduct themselves with professionalism at all times, treating clients with respect, courtesy, and professionalism. This includes being punctual, responsive, and attentive to clients' needs, as well as maintaining confidentiality and discretion in handling sensitive information. By upholding high standards of professionalism, realtors can instill confidence and trust in their clients and enhance the overall client experience.

5. **Proactive Communication:** Proactive communication is key to keeping clients informed, engaged, and reassured throughout the home buying process. Realtors should provide regular updates on market developments, property listings, and progress updates on the transaction. Additionally, realtors should anticipate potential challenges or setbacks and communicate them to clients promptly, along with proposed solutions or mitigation strategies. By staying ahead of the curve and proactively addressing issues, realtors can build credibility and trust with their clients and minimize stress and uncertainty in the home buying journey.

Chapter 9 has underscored the critical importance of effective communication between realtors and loan officers in facilitating successful real estate transactions. From setting clear expectations to managing setbacks and fostering productive working relationships, realtors play a pivotal role in ensuring that clients navigate the complexities of financing with confidence and ease.

By embracing principles of collaboration, transparency, and proactive communication, realtors can leverage their partnership with loan officers to streamline the mortgage process, manage client expectations, and overcome obstacles that may arise along the way. Through insightful guidance and actionable advice, this chapter equips realtors with the tools and knowledge they need to navigate the intricacies of communicating effectively with loan officers, ultimately empowering them to deliver exceptional service and support to their clients throughout the home buying journey.

As you apply the strategies outlined in this chapter in your interactions with loan officers and clients, remember that effective communication is not just about exchanging information—it's about building trust, fostering collaboration, and advocating for your clients' best interests. By prioritizing clear and open communication, you can enhance the client experience, navigate setbacks with confidence, and ultimately, achieve successful outcomes in real estate transactions.

Educating Clients on Mortgage Options

In the intricate landscape of real estate transactions, educating clients on mortgage options stands as a pivotal step towards informed decision-making and successful outcomes. Chapter 10 delves into the essential role of realtors in guiding their clients through the myriad of mortgage choices available to them, ensuring they make well-informed decisions aligned with their financial goals and preferences.

As trusted advisors, realtors serve as invaluable resources for their clients, providing expert guidance and insights into the diverse array of mortgage options tailored to their individual needs. This chapter explores the importance of educating clients on mortgage options, offering strategies and best practices for realtors to effectively communicate complex concepts and empower their clients to navigate the mortgage landscape with confidence.

From conventional loans to government-backed programs, the chapter delves into the various types of mortgage options available to home buyers, highlighting their distinct features, advantages, and considerations. Realtors will gain valuable insights into how to assess their clients' financial profiles and preferences, matching them with the most suitable mortgage products to achieve their homeownership aspirations.

Furthermore, the chapter emphasizes the importance of transparency, clarity, and unbiased guidance in the mortgage education process. Realtors will learn how to demystify mortgage terminology, break down complex concepts, and provide comprehensive information to their clients, fostering trust and confidence in their decision-making journey.

By equipping realtors with the knowledge and tools to educate their clients on mortgage options, Chapter 10 aims to empower them to become trusted advisors and advocates for their clients' financial well-being. Through effective communication, tailored guidance, and a commitment to client empowerment, realtors can ensure their clients make informed decisions that align with their long-term homeownership goals.

Techniques For Educating Clients About Mortgage Loan Options

Educating clients about mortgage loan options is a crucial aspect of the real estate transaction process, and it requires realtors to employ effective techniques to ensure their clients make informed decisions that align with their financial goals and circumstances. We will be exploring various techniques that realtors can utilize to educate their clients about mortgage loan options, with a focus on how these techniques can be applied in their communication with home buyers.

1. **Needs Assessment:** Before delving into specific mortgage loan options, realtors should conduct a comprehensive needs assessment with their clients. This involves understanding their clients' financial situation, long-term goals, risk tolerance, and preferences. By gaining insight into their clients' unique circumstances, realtors can tailor their education efforts to provide relevant information and recommendations.

2. **Simplified Explanation:** Mortgage terminology can be complex and intimidating for many home buyers. Realtors should strive to simplify and explain mortgage loan options in clear, jargon-free language that clients can easily understand. Using analogies, real-life examples, and visual aids can help demystify concepts such as interest rates, loan terms, and repayment options.

3. **Comparison Charts:** Creating comparison charts that outline the features, benefits, and drawbacks of different mortgage loan options can be an effective educational tool for clients. Realtors can use these charts to visually illustrate the differences between loan programs, including factors such as interest rates, down payment requirements, closing costs, and eligibility criteria. This allows clients to make side-by-side comparisons and evaluate which option best suits their needs.

4. **Case Studies:** Sharing real-life case studies or testimonials from past clients who have successfully navigated the mortgage loan process can provide valuable insights and reassurance to current

132

clients. Realtors can highlight specific scenarios where different mortgage loan options were utilized to achieve specific goals, demonstrating the practical application of various loan programs in real-world situations.

5. **Interactive Tools:** Utilizing interactive tools such as mortgage calculators, online quizzes, or virtual simulations can engage clients and enhance their understanding of mortgage loan options. These tools allow clients to input their financial information and explore different scenarios, such as varying loan amounts, interest rates, and repayment terms, to see how they impact monthly payments and overall affordability.

6. **Ongoing Communication:** Effective education about mortgage loan options is not a one-time event but rather an ongoing process throughout the home buying journey. Realtors should maintain regular communication with their clients, providing updates on market trends, changes in loan programs, and opportunities for refinancing or restructuring existing loans. This ensures that clients remain informed and empowered to make informed decisions at every stage of the process.

7. **Collaboration with Loan Officers:** Realtors can enhance their clients' understanding of mortgage loan options by collaborating closely with experienced loan officers. Loan officers can provide additional insights, answer specific questions, and offer personalized guidance tailored to clients' financial profiles. By working together as a cohesive team, realtors and loan officers can provide comprehensive support and education to clients throughout the mortgage loan process.

Educating clients about mortgage loan options requires realtors to employ a variety of techniques that are tailored to their clients' needs and preferences. By simplifying complex concepts, providing visual aids, sharing real-life examples, utilizing interactive tools, maintaining ongoing communication, and collaborating with loan officers, realtors can empower their clients to make informed decisions and achieve their homeownership goals with confidence.

Providing Personalized Guidance Based on Clients' Needs

Providing personalized guidance based on clients' needs and preferences is essential for realtors to effectively assist home buyers in navigating the complex process of selecting the right mortgage loan option. We will be going over the importance of personalized guidance and outline strategies that realtors can employ to tailor their communication with home buyers.

1. **Understanding Clients' Needs:** The first step in providing personalized guidance is to thoroughly understand the needs, goals, and preferences of each client. Realtors should take the time to conduct in-depth consultations with their clients to assess their financial situation, homeownership objectives, risk tolerance, and other relevant factors. By gaining a clear understanding of what matters most to their clients, realtors can tailor their guidance to align with their specific needs and preferences.

2. **Customized Recommendations:** Based on the information gathered during the consultation process, realtors can provide customized recommendations for mortgage loan options that best meet their clients' requirements. This may involve considering factors such as loan amount, down payment size, interest rate preferences, loan term, and eligibility criteria. Realtors should leverage their knowledge of the local real estate market and available loan programs to offer personalized recommendations that are tailored to their clients' unique circumstances.

3. **Explaining Trade-offs:** It's essential for realtors to help their clients understand the trade-offs associated with different mortgage loan options. This includes explaining the pros and cons of various loan features, such as fixed vs. adjustable interest rates, conventional vs. government-backed loans, and different down payment options. By providing clear and transparent explanations of the trade-offs involved, realtors can empower their clients to make informed decisions that align with their priorities.

4. **Flexibility and Adaptability:** Realtors should remain flexible and adaptable in their approach to providing personalized guidance, recognizing that clients' needs and preferences may evolve throughout the home buying process. As clients gain more

information and experience, their priorities may shift, requiring realtors to adjust their recommendations accordingly. By staying attuned to their clients' changing needs and preferences, realtors can continue to provide relevant and personalized guidance at every stage of the home buying journey.

5. **Active Listening:** Effective communication is key to providing personalized guidance, and realtors should practice active listening to truly understand their clients' concerns, questions, and objectives. By listening attentively to their clients' input and feedback, realtors can tailor their guidance to address specific concerns and preferences, fostering a collaborative and trusting relationship. This includes being responsive to client inquiries, providing timely updates, and offering reassurance and support as needed.

6. **Empowering Clients:** Ultimately, the goal of providing personalized guidance is to empower clients to make confident and informed decisions about their mortgage loan options. Realtors should strive to educate their clients about the available choices, clarify any uncertainties or misconceptions, and provide guidance and support throughout the decision-making process. By empowering clients to take an active role in selecting the right mortgage loan option for their needs, realtors can help them achieve their homeownership goals with confidence and peace of mind.

Providing personalized guidance based on clients' needs and preferences is essential for realtors to effectively assist home buyers in selecting the right mortgage loan option. By understanding clients' unique circumstances, offering customized recommendations, explaining trade-offs, remaining flexible and adaptable, practicing active listening, and empowering clients to make informed decisions, realtors can foster a collaborative and trusting relationship that leads to successful outcomes in the home buying process.

Empowering Clients to Make Informed Decisions

Empowering clients to make informed decisions about their mortgage is a crucial aspect of the realtor-client relationship, as it allows home buyers to navigate the complex process of obtaining financing with confidence and clarity. In this part, we will explore the importance of empowering clients and discuss strategies that realtors can use to facilitate informed decision-making.

1. **Education and Information:** One of the most effective ways to empower clients is by providing them with comprehensive education and information about the mortgage process. Realtors should take the time to explain key concepts, terminology, and procedures related to mortgage loans, ensuring that clients have a solid understanding of the various options available to them. This may include discussing different types of loans, interest rates, loan terms, down payment requirements, and closing costs.

2. **Transparent Communication:** Transparent communication is essential for empowering clients to make informed decisions about their mortgage. Realtors should be open and honest with their clients about the benefits and limitations of different loan options, as well as any potential risks or challenges they may encounter along the way. By providing clear and transparent information, realtors can help clients weigh their options and make decisions that align with their financial goals and preferences.

3. **Personalized Guidance:** Every client has unique needs, preferences, and priorities when it comes to selecting a mortgage loan. Realtors should offer personalized guidance that takes into account each client's individual circumstances, such as their budget, credit history, employment status, and long-term homeownership goals. By tailoring their recommendations to meet the specific needs of each client, realtors can empower them to choose the loan option that best suits their needs and objectives.

4. **Encouraging Questions and Feedback:** Empowering clients also involves encouraging them to ask questions, seek clarification, and provide feedback throughout the mortgage process. Realtors should create a supportive and inclusive environment where clients feel comfortable expressing their concerns, voicing their opinions, and participating in the decision-making process. By actively soliciting client input and addressing their questions and concerns in a timely and respectful manner, realtors can foster a sense of trust and confidence in their clients.

5. **Providing Resources and Tools:** Realtors can empower clients by providing them with access to resources and tools that facilitate informed decision-making about their mortgage. This may include educational materials, online calculators, and other resources that help clients understand their financing options, estimate their monthly payments, and compare loan terms from different lenders. By equipping clients with the knowledge and tools they need to make informed decisions, realtors can empower them to take control of their financial future.

6. **Advocacy and Support:** Throughout the mortgage process, realtors should serve as advocates for their clients, representing their best interests and advocating on their behalf with lenders and other parties involved in the transaction. Realtors should provide ongoing support and guidance to clients, helping them navigate any challenges or obstacles that may arise and ensuring that their interests are protected every step of the way. By acting as trusted advisors and advocates, realtors can empower clients to make informed decisions about their mortgage and achieve their homeownership goals with confidence.

Let's reaffirm the pivotal role of realtors in educating their clients about mortgage options, guiding them through the intricate landscape of real estate transactions with expertise and insight. Throughout this chapter, we've emphasized the importance of providing personalized guidance, transparent communication, and empowering clients to make informed decisions aligned with their financial goals and preferences.

From conducting needs assessments to offering customized recommendations, explaining trade-offs, practicing active listening, and providing ongoing support, realtors play a crucial role in empowering their clients to navigate the complexities of the mortgage process with confidence and clarity.

By equipping realtors with effective techniques for educating clients about mortgage loan options, Chapter 9 aims to empower them to become trusted advisors and advocates for their clients' financial well-being. Through tailored guidance, transparent communication, and a commitment to client empowerment, realtors can ensure their clients make informed decisions that lead to successful outcomes in their homeownership journey.

As you apply the strategies outlined in this chapter in your interactions with clients, remember that your role extends beyond mere transaction facilitation—you are a partner, educator, and advocate for your clients' financial future. With the knowledge and tools provided, you are well-equipped to guide your clients through the mortgage process with confidence, empowering them to achieve their homeownership goals and secure their financial well-being.

Chapter 11

Staying Updated on Mortgage Industry Trends

In the dynamic landscape of the real estate market, staying abreast of mortgage industry trends is paramount for realtors seeking to provide exceptional service to their clients. Chapter 11 delves into the importance of staying updated on mortgage industry trends and offers valuable insights and strategies for realtors to remain informed and adaptable in an ever-evolving market.

As the mortgage industry undergoes continual shifts and developments influenced by economic factors, regulatory changes, and emerging technologies, realtors must possess a deep understanding of current trends to effectively navigate challenges and capitalize on opportunities. By staying updated on mortgage industry trends, realtors can anticipate market fluctuations, identify emerging patterns, and adapt their strategies to meet the evolving needs of their clients.

This chapter explores various avenues through which realtors can stay informed about mortgage industry trends, including leveraging industry publications, attending professional development events, networking with industry experts, and utilizing digital resources and technology platforms. Additionally, it provides practical tips and best practices for integrating trend analysis into client consultations, market research, and business planning initiatives.

By embracing a proactive approach to staying updated on mortgage industry trends, realtors can enhance their credibility, competence, and competitiveness in the real estate market. This chapter equips realtors with the knowledge and tools necessary to navigate the complexities of the mortgage industry with confidence and adaptability, ultimately empowering them to deliver exceptional value and service to their clients.

Staying Informed about Changes in the Mortgage Industry

In the dynamic realm of real estate, particularly within the mortgage industry, change is the only constant. Economic shifts, regulatory updates, technological advancements, and market trends continuously reshape the landscape, impacting borrowers, lenders, and real estate professionals alike. For realtors, staying informed about these changes is not merely advantageous—it's essential for providing top-tier service to home buyers. This section explores the critical importance of staying informed about changes in the mortgage industry and how realtors can leverage this knowledge when communicating with home buyers.

1. **Understanding Market Dynamics**: Changes in the mortgage industry can significantly influence market dynamics, affecting factors such as interest rates, loan availability, and borrowing costs. By staying informed about these changes, realtors can offer valuable insights to home buyers regarding market conditions, helping them make informed decisions about when to buy, sell, or refinance.

2. **Advising on Financing Options**: With a thorough understanding of mortgage industry changes, realtors can effectively advise home buyers on financing options that align with their financial goals and circumstances. Whether it's navigating new loan programs, understanding eligibility requirements, or anticipating shifts in interest rates, realtors can provide tailored guidance to help clients secure the most advantageous financing arrangements.

3. **Mitigating Risks**: Changes in mortgage regulations and lending practices can introduce new risks and challenges for home buyers. Realtors who stay informed about these changes can help clients navigate potential pitfalls, ensuring compliance with regulatory requirements and minimizing the risk of encountering issues during the loan application process.

4. **Building Trust and Credibility**: Home buyers rely on realtors as trusted advisors throughout the home buying journey. By demonstrating a deep understanding of mortgage industry changes, realtors can enhance their credibility and build trust with clients. This positions realtors as knowledgeable experts

who are equipped to guide clients through the complexities of the mortgage process with confidence.

5. **Anticipating Client Needs**: Informed realtors are better equipped to anticipate client needs and proactively address questions or concerns related to mortgage financing. By staying ahead of industry trends and developments, realtors can provide timely and relevant information to clients, fostering a smoother and more transparent home buying experience.

6. **Navigating Competitive Markets**: In competitive real estate markets, having up-to-date knowledge of mortgage industry changes can provide a competitive edge. Realtors who are well-informed about the latest lending products, interest rate trends, and financing options can offer strategic advice to help clients stand out in competitive bidding situations and secure their desired properties.

Staying informed about changes in the mortgage industry is paramount for realtors seeking to provide exceptional service to home buyers. By understanding market dynamics, advising on financing options, mitigating risks, building trust and credibility, anticipating client needs, and navigating competitive markets, realtors can leverage their knowledge to empower clients and facilitate successful real estate transactions. In an ever-evolving industry, the ability to stay informed and adapt to change is key to achieving success as a real estate professional.

Resources for Realtors to Stay Updated on Mortgage Trends

In the fast-paced world of real estate, staying informed about mortgage trends is essential for realtors to provide valuable guidance and support to their clients. With constant changes in interest rates, lending policies, and market conditions, realtors must rely on a variety of resources and tools to stay updated on mortgage trends. This essay explores some of the most valuable resources and tools available to realtors and how they can use this information to effectively communicate with home buyers.

1. **Industry Publications and News Outlets**: Realtors can stay abreast of mortgage trends by regularly reading industry publications and news outlets dedicated to real estate and finance. Publications such as Realtor Magazine, Mortgage Professional America, and The Mortgage Reports provide valuable insights into market trends, regulatory changes, and industry developments. By staying informed through these sources, realtors can better understand the factors influencing mortgage trends and communicate this information to home buyers.

2. **Professional Associations and Organizations**: Membership in professional associations and organizations related to real estate and mortgage lending can provide realtors with access to valuable resources and networking opportunities. Associations such as the National Association of Realtors (NAR), the Mortgage Bankers Association (MBA), and the National Association of Mortgage Brokers (NAMB) often offer educational resources, webinars, and conferences focused on mortgage trends and industry updates. Realtors can leverage these resources to stay informed and exchange knowledge with peers and industry experts.

3. **Training and Continuing Education Programs**: Many real estate brokerages and training organizations offer specialized training and continuing education programs focused on mortgage trends and financing options. Realtors can enroll in courses covering topics such as mortgage financing, loan programs, and regulatory compliance to deepen their understanding of the mortgage industry. By investing in ongoing education, realtors can stay ahead of the curve and provide expert guidance to their clients on mortgage-related matters.

4. **Online Resources and Blogs**: The internet is a treasure trove of information on mortgage trends, with numerous blogs, forums, and websites dedicated to real estate and finance. Realtors can follow reputable online resources such as Zillow Research, Redfin Insights, and Bankrate to access market reports, economic forecasts, and mortgage rate updates. Additionally, participating in online forums and discussion groups can provide realtors with valuable insights and perspectives from industry professionals and fellow real estate practitioners.

5. **Networking with Lenders and Mortgage Professionals**: Building relationships with lenders, mortgage brokers, and loan officers can be invaluable for realtors seeking to stay updated on mortgage trends. By networking with mortgage professionals, realtors can gain firsthand knowledge of lending practices, loan products, and market trends. Collaborating with trusted mortgage partners allows realtors to access insider information and provide clients with tailored financing solutions that meet their needs.

6. **Data Analytics and Market Research Tools**: Realtors can leverage data analytics and market research tools to track mortgage trends and market conditions in real-time. Platforms such as CoreLogic, Black Knight, and ATTOM Data Solutions provide comprehensive data on home sales, mortgage originations, and foreclosure rates, allowing realtors to identify emerging trends and patterns in the housing market. By analyzing this data, realtors can make informed decisions and advise clients on timing their home purchase or sale based on prevailing mortgage trends.

Realtors have access to a wealth of resources and tools to stay updated on mortgage trends and provide valuable guidance to their clients. By leveraging industry publications, professional associations, training programs, online resources, networking opportunities, and data analytics tools, realtors can stay ahead of the curve and offer expert advice on mortgage-related matters. In an ever-evolving real estate landscape, staying informed and proactive is essential for realtors to excel in their role as trusted advisors to home buyers.

Adapting to Evolving Market Conditions and Regulations

In the dynamic landscape of real estate, market conditions and regulations are in a perpetual state of flux. Economic shifts, regulatory updates, and emerging trends continually reshape the industry, presenting both challenges and opportunities for realtors. To thrive in this ever-changing environment, realtors must employ effective strategies for adapting to evolving market conditions and regulations. This explores key strategies for realtors to navigate changes in the real estate landscape and leverage this information when communicating with home buyers.

1. **Continuous Learning and Education**: In an industry as dynamic as real estate, knowledge is power. Realtors must prioritize ongoing learning and education to stay abreast of evolving market conditions, regulatory changes, and industry trends. Participating in professional development programs, attending industry conferences, and earning relevant certifications can equip realtors with the knowledge and skills needed to adapt to change effectively.

2. **Stay Informed through Industry Publications and News**: Realtors should make it a habit to stay informed about industry news and developments through reputable publications, websites, and news sources. Subscribing to industry newsletters, following real estate blogs, and staying active on professional networking platforms can provide valuable insights into market trends, regulatory updates, and emerging issues.

3. **Leverage Technology and Data Analytics**: Technology plays an increasingly vital role in the real estate industry, offering realtors powerful tools for analyzing market data, identifying trends, and making informed decisions. Realtors can leverage technology platforms and data analytics tools to track market indicators, assess property values, and gain insights into buyer preferences. By harnessing the power of technology, realtors can adapt more effectively to evolving market conditions and provide valuable insights to home buyers.

4. **Build Strong Relationships with Industry Professionals**: Realtors should cultivate strong relationships with industry professionals, including mortgage lenders, attorneys, appraisers, and inspectors. These relationships can provide realtors with valuable insights into market trends, regulatory changes, and emerging issues, enabling them to adapt more effectively to evolving conditions. Collaborating with trusted professionals can also facilitate smoother transactions and provide additional support to home buyers.

5. **Adapt Communication Strategies**: As market conditions and regulations evolve, realtors must adapt their communication strategies to effectively convey information to home buyers. This may involve simplifying complex concepts, providing clear explanations of regulatory changes, and offering guidance on navigating shifting market dynamics. By tailoring their communication strategies to meet the needs of home buyers,

realtors can ensure that clients are well-informed and confident in their decisions.

6. **Maintain Flexibility and Adaptability**: In an ever-changing industry, flexibility and adaptability are essential traits for realtors. Realtors must be prepared to pivot quickly in response to changing market conditions, regulatory requirements, and client needs. By maintaining flexibility and embracing change, realtors can position themselves as trusted advisors who can navigate the complexities of the real estate landscape with ease.

As we conclude Chapter 11, we reaffirm the vital importance of staying updated on mortgage industry trends in the dynamic world of real estate. Throughout this chapter, we've explored how continual shifts and developments influenced by economic factors, regulatory changes, and emerging technologies shape the mortgage landscape. It's evident that realtors must possess a deep understanding of current trends to effectively navigate challenges and capitalize on opportunities for their clients.

From understanding market dynamics to advising on financing options, mitigating risks, building trust, and navigating competitive markets, staying informed about changes in the mortgage industry is paramount for providing exceptional service to homebuyers. By embracing a proactive approach to staying updated on mortgage industry trends, realtors can enhance their credibility, competence, and competitiveness in the real estate market.

We've provided a plethora of resources and tools for realtors to stay updated, including leveraging industry publications, attending professional development events, networking with experts, and utilizing digital resources. Additionally, we've emphasized the practical integration of trend analysis into client consultations, market research, and business planning initiatives.

In an ever-evolving industry, the ability to adapt and innovate is key to achieving success as a real estate professional. By employing effective strategies such as continuous learning, leveraging technology, building strong relationships, adapting communication strategies, and maintaining flexibility, realtors can thrive amidst evolving market conditions and regulations.

As you embark on your journey in the real estate world, remember that staying informed about mortgage industry trends isn't just about keeping up—it's about staying ahead and empowering yourself to deliver exceptional value and service to your clients. With the knowledge and tools provided in this chapter, you are equipped to navigate the complexities of the mortgage industry with confidence and adaptability, ensuring success in your endeavors as a trusted advisor in the realm of real estate.

Chapter 12

To Wrap Things Up

As we approach the end of our comprehensive guide, designed explicitly for realtors on the complex landscape of mortgage lending, it is essential to recognize the significance of the journey we have embarked upon together. This final chapter serves as a capstone, synthesizing the wealth of knowledge, strategies, and insights we have explored to equip you, the realtor, with an unparalleled understanding of guiding clients through the home buying process. The intricacies of mortgage lending, which can often appear daunting to both realtors and their clients, have been unraveled to reveal a structured and navigable path towards successful homeownership.

Our exploration has been meticulous and wide-ranging, covering the spectrum of mortgage loan types, understanding appraisal challenges, addressing loan denials, and the indispensable pre-approval process. These topics have been dissected with a focus on technical knowledge and practical application, ensuring that you are equipped not just with information but with actionable strategies that can be applied in real-world scenarios.

This final chapter aims to encapsulate the main points covered, highlight essential concepts and strategies, and remind you of key insights and practical tips that will serve as your compass in the real estate industry. It's designed to reinforce your understanding and confidence in navigating mortgage lending processes, enabling you to offer unparalleled guidance and support to your clients.

Pre-approval, documentation, effective communication, and understanding the dynamics of creditworthiness and interest rates are just a few of the cornerstones that have been emphasized throughout our discussions. These elements are critical in fostering smooth transactions, building trust among stakeholders, and ultimately, in achieving successful closings.

Moreover, this chapter acknowledges the dynamic and ever-evolving nature of the mortgage lending and real estate landscape. It underscores the importance of staying informed about industry trends, regulatory changes, and technological advancements that can impact the mortgage process. Adaptability and a commitment to continuous learning are highlighted as vital attributes for realtors aspiring to maintain their competitive edge and provide the best possible service to their clients.

As we wrap up this comprehensive guide, it is my hope that the insights and knowledge shared will not only serve as a valuable resource in your professional toolkit but will also inspire a deeper commitment to excellence and client service. The role of a realtor in the mortgage process is pivotal—bridging the gap between clients' homeownership dreams and the complex realities of mortgage lending. With the strategies, insights, and practical tips outlined in this guide, you are now better equipped to navigate these challenges, advocate for your clients, and contribute to their journey toward successful homeownership with confidence and expertise.

Let this final chapter serve not just as a conclusion but as a springboard into the future, where the principles and strategies you have learned guide your actions and interactions in the real estate market. Empowered with knowledge and driven by a commitment to your clients' success, you are poised to make a significant impact in the lives of those you serve and in the broader landscape of the real estate industry.

Summary of the Main Points Covered

Throughout our comprehensive exploration, we've traversed a diverse landscape of critical topics that underpin the intricate world of mortgage lending in real estate transactions. From the foundational understanding of the multitude of mortgage loan types to the nuanced strategies for addressing appraisal challenges and navigating through loan denials, our journey has been both enlightening and practical.

We've underscored the pivotal role of pre-approval as the cornerstone of a successful home buying process, illuminating its significance in streamlining transactions and empowering buyers with a clear understanding of their purchasing power. Emphasizing the meticulous attention to documentation, we've highlighted how comprehensive and accurate paperwork serves as the bedrock of a smooth mortgage application, minimizing delays and facilitating efficient processing.

Effective communication emerges as a recurring theme throughout our exploration, serving as the linchpin that binds together various stakeholders in the real estate ecosystem. By fostering open channels of communication between buyers, realtors, and lenders, we've emphasized how clarity, transparency, and responsiveness pave the way for seamless transactions and foster trust and confidence among all parties involved.

Key insights into the critical role of creditworthiness in securing favorable loan terms, the dynamic interplay of interest rates in shaping borrowing costs, and the nuanced understanding of market conditions' influence on mortgage lending decisions have equipped realtors with a comprehensive toolkit for navigating the ever-evolving landscape of real estate financing.

In essence, our exploration has illuminated the multifaceted nature of mortgage lending, providing realtors with a robust foundation of knowledge, skills, and strategies to navigate the complexities of the mortgage process with confidence and proficiency. As we reflect on the breadth and depth of our journey, we're reminded of the profound impact that mastery of mortgage lending principles can have on facilitating successful real estate transactions and empowering clients to achieve their homeownership dreams.

Highlights of Essential Concepts and Strategies

Our exploration has illuminated a plethora of essential concepts and strategies that form the bedrock of success in the realm of mortgage lending within the real estate landscape. From foundational concepts to advanced strategies, we've delved into a rich tapestry of knowledge designed to empower realtors with the tools and insights needed to navigate the complexities of the mortgage process effectively.

At the core of our discussion lie fundamental concepts such as fixed-rate and adjustable-rate mortgages, FHA and VA loans, and the distinction between conventional and non-conventional loans. By elucidating the intricacies of each loan type, we've equipped realtors with a nuanced understanding of the diverse array of financing options available to home buyers, enabling them to tailor their recommendations to best suit their clients' unique needs and preferences.

Moreover, our exploration has extended beyond mere theoretical understanding to practical strategies aimed at mitigating risks and overcoming challenges encountered throughout the mortgage process. From navigating appraisal discrepancies to addressing loan denials and other setbacks, we've provided realtors with a comprehensive toolkit of strategies designed to navigate obstacles with finesse and resilience, ensuring the smooth progression of real estate transactions.

Central to our discussion is the importance of fostering productive relationships with loan officers, recognizing their pivotal role in facilitating successful transactions. By establishing open lines of communication and fostering a spirit of collaboration, realtors can leverage the expertise and resources of loan officers to navigate the intricacies of the mortgage process with confidence and efficiency.

Furthermore, our exploration has underscored the critical role of education in empowering clients to make informed decisions about their mortgage options. By equipping realtors with the knowledge and communication skills needed to educate clients about the intricacies of mortgage lending, we've empowered them to serve as trusted advisors, guiding clients through the complexities of the mortgage process with clarity and confidence.

Finally, we've emphasized the importance of staying updated on industry trends and adapting to evolving market conditions. In an ever-changing landscape, staying informed and agile is essential for realtors seeking to maintain a competitive edge and provide the highest level of service to their clients. By remaining vigilant and proactive in monitoring industry trends and regulatory changes, realtors can position themselves as trusted advisors, capable of navigating the dynamic currents of the real estate market with skill and expertise.

Reminders of Key Insights and Practical Tips for Realtors

As we conclude our journey through the intricacies of mortgage lending in the real estate realm, it's crucial to revisit key insights and practical tips that serve as guiding principles for realtors in their daily practice. These reminders encapsulate the essence of our exploration, offering invaluable wisdom to inform and enrich realtors' interactions with clients and stakeholders alike.

First and foremost, we underscore the importance of pre-approval as a foundational step in the home buying process. By encouraging clients to obtain pre-approval for a mortgage, realtors can empower them with a clear understanding of their purchasing power and streamline the search for their dream home. Pre-approval not only enhances clients' credibility as serious buyers but also expedites the transaction process by providing sellers with the assurance of financial readiness.

Accurate documentation emerges as another cornerstone of success in the mortgage process, serving as the linchpin of transparency and trust between all parties involved. Realtors must emphasize the meticulous gathering and submission of all required documents, ensuring compliance with lender guidelines and regulatory requirements. By prioritizing accuracy and completeness in documentation, realtors can mitigate the risk of delays and setbacks, facilitating a seamless transaction experience for their clients.

The value of open communication cannot be overstated in the context of real estate transactions. Realtors must maintain transparent and frequent communication with clients, loan officers, and other stakeholders throughout the mortgage process. Clear and timely communication fosters trust, minimizes misunderstandings, and enables swift resolution of any issues or concerns that may arise along the way. By serving as proactive communicators and advocates for their clients' interests, realtors can instill confidence and peace of mind in their clientele.
In addition to these foundational principles, our exploration has provided realtors with practical insights and strategies for addressing common challenges encountered in the mortgage process. Whether navigating credit issues, appraisal discrepancies, or loan denials, realtors are equipped with a toolkit of strategies designed to overcome obstacles with poise and determination. By leveraging these insights and techniques, realtors can navigate the complexities of the mortgage process with confidence, guiding their clients to successful outcomes and fulfilling their dreams of homeownership.

As we draw the curtains on this comprehensive guide to mortgage lending tailored for realtors, it becomes paramount to internalize and apply the wealth of knowledge and insights gained throughout our exploration. This isn't just the end of a chapter; it's a pivotal moment to propel your professional practice to new heights by harnessing the power of these key takeaways.

By incorporating the insights gleaned from this book into your daily interactions and transactions, realtors have the opportunity to elevate their effectiveness and efficacy in serving clients' needs. Armed with a deeper understanding of mortgage lending nuances, realtors can navigate the complexities of the real estate landscape with finesse and confidence.

Moreover, the strategies outlined in this book serve as invaluable tools for building stronger relationships not only with clients but also with lenders and other industry stakeholders. By fostering collaborative partnerships and open lines of communication, realtors can cultivate a network of support that enhances their ability to deliver exceptional service and results for their clientele.

Ultimately, the goal is to translate this newfound knowledge into tangible success in facilitating real estate transactions. Whether it's guiding clients through the mortgage process, advocating on their behalf with lenders, or navigating unforeseen challenges, realtors equipped with the insights from this guide are poised to achieve greater levels of success and satisfaction in their professional endeavors.

As you embark on the next chapter of your journey in the real estate industry, remember to carry forward these key takeaways and insights as guiding principles. Embrace continuous learning, adaptability, and a commitment to excellence, and watch as you unlock new opportunities for growth and achievement in your career as a realtor.

Government Mortgage Information Sources

Consumer Financial Protection Bureau (CFPB)
- Website: www.consumerfinance.gov/mortgage
- Phone: 1-855-411-2372

Federal Housing Administration (FHA)
- Website: www.fha.gov
- Phone: 1-800-CALL-FHA (1-800-225-5342)

Freddie Mac
- Website: www.freddiemac.com
- Phone: 1-800-FREDDIE (1-800-373-3343)

Fannie Mae
- Website: www.fanniemae.com
- Phone: 1-800-2FANNIE (1-800-232-6643)

Department of Housing and Urban Development (HUD)
- Website: www.hud.gov
- Phone: 1-800-CALL-FHA (1-800-225-5342)

U.S. Department of Agriculture (USDA) Rural Development
- Website: www.rd.usda.gov
- Phone: 1-800-414-1226

Department of Veterans Affairs (VA) Home Loans
- Website: www.benefits.va.gov/homeloans
- Phone: 1-877-827-3702

Consumer Financial Protection Bureau (CFPB) Mortgage Assistance Programs
- Website: www.consumerfinance.gov/owning-a-home/mortgage-assistance
- Phone: 1-855-411-2372

Federal Trade Commission (FTC) Mortgage Information
- Website: www.consumer.ftc.gov/topics/mortgages
- Phone: 1-877-FTC-HELP (1-877-382-4357)

U.S. Department of Housing and Urban Development (HUD) Counseling Agencies
- Website: www.hud.gov/offices/hsg/sfh/hcc/hcs.cfm
- Phone: 1-800-569-4287

U.S. Department of Justice (DOJ) Fair Lending Division
- Website: www.justice.gov/crt/fair-housing-act-2

- Phone: 1-800-896-7743

U.S. Department of Treasury Mortgage Assistance Programs

- Website: www.treasury.gov/initiatives/financial-stability/TARP-Programs/housing/Pages/default.aspx
- Phone: 1-888-995-HOPE (1-888-995-4673)

State Mortgage Information Sources

1. **Alabama**
   - Alabama Banking Department
     - Website: www.banking.alabama.gov
     - Phone: (334) 242-3452
2. **Alaska**
   - Alaska Division of Banking and Securities
     - Website: www.commerce.alaska.gov/web/dbs
     - Phone: (907) 269-8140
3. **Arizona**
   - Arizona Department of Financial Institutions
     - Website: www.azdfi.gov
     - Phone: (602) 771-2800
4. **Arkansas**
   - Arkansas Securities Department
     - Website: www.securities.arkansas.gov
     - Phone: (501) 324-9260
5. **California**
   - California Department of Real Estate (DRE)
     - Website: www.dre.ca.gov
     - Phone: (877) 373-4542
6. **Colorado**
   - Colorado Division of Real Estate
     - Website: www.colorado.gov/dora/division-real-estate
     - Phone: (303) 894-2166
7. **Connecticut**
   - Connecticut Department of Banking
     - Website: portal.ct.gov/DOB
     - Phone: (860) 240-8170
8. **Delaware**
   - Delaware Office of the State Bank Commissioner
     - Website: banking.delaware.gov
     - Phone: (302) 739-4235
9. **Florida**
   - Florida Office of Financial Regulation (OFR)
     - Website: www.flofr.com

- Phone: (850) 487-9687

10. **Georgia**
    - Georgia Department of Banking and Finance
        - Website: dbf.georgia.gov
        - Phone: (770) 986-1136

11. **Hawaii**
    - Hawaii Division of Financial Institutions
        - Website: cca.hawaii.gov/dfi
        - Phone: (808) 586-2820

12. **Idaho**
    - Idaho Department of Finance
        - Website: finance.idaho.gov
        - Phone: (208) 332-8000

13. **Illinois**
    - Illinois Department of Financial and Professional Regulation (IDFPR)
        - Website: www.idfpr.com
        - Phone: (800) 560-6420

14. **Indiana**
    - Indiana Department of Financial Institutions
        - Website: www.in.gov/dfi
        - Phone: (317) 232-3955

15. **Iowa**
    - Iowa Division of Banking
        - Website: www.idob.state.ia.us
        - Phone: (515) 281-4014

16. **Kansas**
    - Office of the State Bank Commissioner of Kansas
        - Website: www.osbckansas.org
        - Phone: (785) 296-2266

17. **Kentucky**
    - Kentucky Department of Financial Institutions
        - Website: www.kfi.ky.gov
        - Phone: (800) 223-2579

18. **Louisiana**
    - Louisiana Office of Financial Institutions
        - Website: www.ofi.la.gov
        - Phone: (225) 925-4660

19. **Maine**
    - Maine Bureau of Consumer Credit Protection
        - Website: www.maine.gov/pfr/consumercredit/index.shtml
        - Phone: (207) 624-8527

20. **Maryland**

- Maryland Department of Labor, Licensing and Regulation
  - Website: www.dllr.state.md.us
  - Phone: (410) 230-6100

21. **Massachusetts**
    - Massachusetts Division of Banks
      - Website: www.mass.gov/orgs/division-of-banks
      - Phone: (617) 956-1500

22. **Michigan**
    - Michigan Department of Insurance and Financial Services (DIFS)
      - Website: www.michigan.gov/difs
      - Phone: (877) 999-6442

23. **Minnesota**
    - Minnesota Department of Commerce
      - Website: mn.gov/commerce
      - Phone: (651) 539-1500

24. **Mississippi**
    - Mississippi Department of Banking and Consumer Finance
      - Website: www.dbcf.ms.gov
      - Phone: (601) 321-6901

25. **Missouri**
    - Missouri Division of Finance
      - Website: finance.mo.gov
      - Phone: (573) 751-3242

26. **Montana**
    - Montana Division of Banking and Financial Institutions
      - Website: banking.mt.gov
      - Phone: (406) 841-2920

27. **Nebraska**
    - Nebraska Department of Banking and Finance
      - Website: www.ndbf.nebraska.gov
      - Phone: (402) 471-2171

28. **Nevada**
    - Nevada Division of Mortgage Lending
      - Website: mld.nv.gov
      - Phone: (702) 486-0782

29. **New Hampshire**
    - New Hampshire Banking Department
      - Website: www.nh.gov/banking
      - Phone: (603) 271-3561

30. **New Jersey**
    - New Jersey Department of Banking and Insurance

- Website: www.state.nj.us/dobi/index.html
- Phone: (609) 292-7272

31. **New Mexico**
    - New Mexico Financial Institutions Division
        - Website: www.rld.state.nm.us/financialinstitutions
        - Phone: (505) 476-4885

32. **New York**
    - New York State Department of Financial Services (DFS)
        - Website: www.dfs.ny.gov
        - Phone: (800) 342-3736

33. **North Carolina**
    - North Carolina Commissioner of Banks
        - Website: www.nccob.gov
        - Phone: (919) 733-3016

34. **North Dakota**
    - North Dakota Department of Financial Institutions
        - Website: www.nd.gov/dfi
        - Phone: (701) 328-9933

35. **Ohio**
    - Ohio Department of Commerce Division of Real Estate & Professional Licensing
        - Website: www.com.ohio.gov/real
        - Phone: (614) 466-4100

36. **Oklahoma**
    - Oklahoma Department of Consumer Credit
        - Website: www.ok.gov/okdocc
        - Phone: (405) 521-3653

37. **Oregon**
    - Oregon Division of Financial Regulation
        - Website: dfr.oregon.gov
        - Phone: (503) 378-4140

38. **Pennsylvania**
    - Pennsylvania Department of Banking and Securities
        - Website: www.dobs.pa.gov
        - Phone: (800) 722-2657

39. **Rhode Island**
    - Rhode Island Department of Business Regulation
        - Website: www.dbr.ri.gov
        - Phone: (401) 462-9500

40. **South Carolina**
    - South Carolina Department of Consumer Affairs
        - Website: www.consumer.sc.gov
        - Phone: (803) 734-4200

41. **South Dakota**
   - South Dakota Division of Banking
     - Website: dlr.sd.gov/banking
     - Phone: (605) 773-3421
42. **Tennessee**
   - Tennessee Department of Financial Institutions
     - Website: www.tn.gov/tdfi
     - Phone: (615) 741-2236
43. **Texas**
   - Texas Department of Savings and Mortgage Lending
     - Website: www.sml.texas.gov
     - Phone: (512) 475-1350
44. **Utah**
   - Utah Division of Real Estate
     - Website: realestate.utah.gov
     - Phone: (801) 530-6747
45. **Vermont**
   - Vermont Department of Financial Regulation
     - Website: dfr.vermont.gov
     - Phone: (802) 828-3301
46. **Virginia**
   - Virginia Bureau of Financial Institutions
     - Website: www.scc.virginia.gov/bfi
     - Phone: (804) 371-9657
47. **Washington**
   - Washington State Department of Financial Institutions
     - Website: dfi.wa.gov
     - Phone: (360) 902-8700
48. **West Virginia**
   - West Virginia Division of Financial Institutions
     - Website: www.dfi.wv.gov
     - Phone: (304) 558-2294
49. **Wisconsin**
   - Wisconsin Department of Financial Institutions
     - Website: www.wdfi.org
     - Phone: (608) 261-9555
50. **Wyoming**
   - Wyoming Division of Banking
     - Website: audit.state.wy.us/banking
     - Phone: (307) 777-7797

About the Author

Corey Ramsey, a seasoned professional in the real estate industry, brings a wealth of knowledge and experience to the realm of mortgage financing. With years of dedicated service as a licensed Loan Originator, He has earned a reputation for excellence in guiding clients through the intricacies of property transactions, including mortgage loan programs and options.

Throughout his career, Corey has remained committed to staying abreast of industry trends, regulatory changes, and best practices in real estate finance. He has leveraged his extensive network of industry connections to provide clients with access to a wide range of mortgage products tailored to their unique needs and financial goals.

Corey is excited to share his expertise and insights in "The Realtor's Mortgage Companion" to empower readers with the knowledge and confidence to navigate the mortgage application process successfully. Through his comprehensive guide, he aims to demystify mortgage financing and equip Realtors with the tools they need to make informed decisions on their path to homeownership.

For more information about Corey and his work, please visit WWW.RamseyMortgages.com